Village to
Village

IMPRINT

Village to Village

MISADVENTURES IN FRANCE

ALISTER KERSHAW

Illustrations by
Robin Wallace-Crabbe

Angus&Robertson
An imprint of HarperCollins*Publishers*

An Angus & Robertson Publication

Angus&Robertson, an imprint of
HarperCollins*Publishers*
25 Ryde Road, Pymble, Sydney, NSW 2073, Australia
31 View Road, Glenfield, Auckland 10, New Zealand

First published by Angus & Robertson Publishers, Australia, 1993

National Library of Australia
Cataloguing-in-Publication data:
    Kershaw, Alister, 1921-
    Village to village: misadventures in France.

    ISBN 0 207 17612 4

    I. Kershaw, Alister, 1921-   - Biography. 2. Poets, Australian -
    France - Biography. I. Title.

A821.3

Cover photograph: David Barnes supplied by Stockshots

Typeset by Midland Typesetters, Maryborough, Victoria
Printed by Griffin Paperbacks, Adelaide

9 8 7 6 5 4 3 2 1
96 95 94 93

For Solange

CHAPTER ONE

It was love at first sight and I was astonished that it should be happening to me because the first sight had nothing in the least alluring about it. The roads from airports to cities rarely do. I was like a man who bewilders his friends by becoming infatuated with a particularly unprepossessing woman—warts and a squint and a harelip. 'What on earth does he see in her?' I've often wondered myself. What *did* I see in that dreary road which was taking me to Paris?

This sudden incomprehensible love affair might have been a little less mysterious if I had arrived in France with goose-flesh anticipations of romantic garrets and dangerous liaisons in them, the Latin Quarter and champagne at five francs a bottle, and artists' studios—all the preposterous sentimental paraphernalia from absinthe to *midinettes*. But I had not included any of these notions in my meagre luggage, I had no preliminary yearnings towards the country. Rather the contrary. In Australia I had spent much of my time with a young woman who had visited France just before the war and had gone down with a bad attack of what someone called 'French flu'. She babbled so fervently and persistently about France and Paris that she infected me with a perverse loathing for both.

The fact nonetheless inexplicably remains. A hundred yards from the airport we passed a café ('Le Looping', with the two o's aerobatically askew to make the point clear) and puppy love overwhelmed me—puppy love from which this old dog has not yet shaken himself free. 'Le Looping' and the handful of unremarkable customers sipping their drinks on the terrace instantaneously bewitched me.

I knew, with no rational justification, that I was in a country which for me was unlike any other country. It was as though some indigenous evangelist had caused me to be 'born again'.

One life abruptly ended and another began. There and then I shed my twenty-five years. To this day, in my own head and heart I am twenty-five years younger than the miserable reality.

The passengers in the airport bus were a drab lot. It was only eighteen months since the war had ended. There had not been much time to spruce up. In my besotted state, they seemed to me as fabulous as troubadours. The houses along the road were dismal little pavilions badly in need of a coat of paint. I gaped at them as if each one were the Château de Versailles. And in the distance the Eiffel Tower looked so impossibly like itself as depicted on a thousand postcards and a thousand amateur paintings that the sense of unreality which I had been feeling deepened still further.

What had brought me to Paris was my eagerness to visit a writer I had admired since my school days. He and his wife were to become two of my closest friends. We saw a great deal of each other in the years ahead—in Paris, in the South of France, in the Loire Valley. Of all the countless occasions on which we laughed together, argued, drank wine, loafed on a Mediterranean beach, listened to music, none was as sheerly magical as that first evening in Paris.

Our relationship took shape from the very beginning. We were already friends by the time we left their studio and strolled together down the Boulevard de Montparnasse. For some reason, twilight in Paris, then at least, was not like twilight in any other city. It enveloped you in a wonderful blue and golden luminosity and it had its own special unidentifiable perfume. That one-and-only twilight dreamily descending on us was so unlike anything I had known that I had my first vague glimpse of a mystery which was to become more and more apparent as time went by: Paris was the city of the unexpected. You always felt as though something extraordinary were about to happen. Sometimes it did, sometimes not; but the expectation never diminished. One went on waiting.

Twilight aside, most things were in short supply in 1947. Fortunately, the writer had been familiar with Paris for thirty years or more. He was already on the right sort of terms with the proprietor of an unassuming restaurant in one of the side streets. So we were served with a mixture of raw vegetables, a sorrel omelette (I can still recall the metallic taste of that sorrel) and, thanks to the proprietor's peasant brother, some wild duck. The wine was a muscular red with a powerful rasp to it but (a symptom of French flu?) I thought I had never drunk anything so delicious. It was served in cups as if we were in the prohibition speakeasy era because otherwise less privileged customers would have been clamouring for some and there wasn't any too much to be had.

Afterwards we walked back along the boulevard towards the studio. We stopped midway for a glass of brandy at the Dôme. Tourists had not yet ventured to return to Paris. The other customers on the terrace were all French, completely nondescript but fascinating because they were French. There were practically no cars on the roads. Those there were either had great charcoal-burning furnaces fixed to the back or carried dirigible-like bags of gas on their roofs. Every so often a fiacre went clip-clopping past. The air was almost startling pure. The stars were sharply visible in a translucent sky. I turned to the man at the next table and asked him for a light—speaking French for the first time in my life. I managed to make three ludicrous grammatical blunders in the course of that one short sentence. If he was amused by my linguistic ineptitude he was too polite to show it. *La politesse francaise*—that still existed, too.

I don't have to make an effort to recapture the enchantment of Paris as it was then. I don't have to recapture it at all because it has never left me. The Occupation had had one good effect at least. It had stopped progress dead in its horrible juggernaut tracks. The city had remained unchanged since 1939. Whole districts had remained unchanged since long before that. Old photographs taken around the turn of the century showed streets in which every feature was still recognisably the same. Urban planners and architects scampering after a freakish design to awe the fashionable boobies had not yet been let loose. Politicians had not yet started erecting monuments to their own glory, as hideous as themselves. The first time I saw Paris was practically the last time anyone saw it.

Disenchantment might have succeeded my first raptures. It didn't. Far from it. I became more and more lovesick with a love devoid of any reservations. Paris was totally without blemishes in my eyes. I didn't notice the warts and the squint. I loved all sorts of incongruous trivia. I loved the early-morning noises—tables and chairs being set out on the café terraces, shutters being opened along the street, the grumbling of the first métro like some underground beast roused from hibernation. I loved the policemen's capes and *képis* and the smell of black French tobacco and the uncomfortable metal seats in the Luxembourg Gardens and the cheese merchant leading his flock of goats and luring them on with a strange little tune played on a panpipe.

Street singers, I discovered, could still assemble a ring of listeners. No one was in too much of a hurry to stop for a while. Their repertoire of sentimental or melancholy little songs was pretty much as it had been back in the 1930s, back in the 1920s. Afterwards they sold the sheet music to their audience. Coins thrown from the surrounding windows clinked on the pavement.

Wandering haphazardly around I came on obscure courtyards and alleys in which artisans were working at tasks I had never known existed—manufacturing by hand brass nails to be used in restoring antique furniture, piercing holes in pearls, stringing them (a separate craft), moulding fantastical masks, making wigs out of human hair, carving pipebowls out of ivory. I discovered the *passages*, the covered arcades—the Passage Choiseul and the Passage Vivienne and the rest of them. They were lined with odd little shops which looked as though they had the same stock as they had had in 1900. The few customers looked as though they, too, had been there since 1900.

Above all, I surrendered wholeheartedly to the peculiar spell of Paris cafés. There are probably only half as many now as there were forty years ago. Then there seemed to be one every hundred yards or so. The Australian pubs I had been used to were places where you went for a drink. You didn't actually sleep in the cafés (although one charitable proprietor did actually allow me to do just that when I had nowhere else to go) but for the rest you virtually lived there.

Some of the cafés were too like Kubla Khan's stately pleasure dome for my taste but these were in the minority. The bulk of them—and these were the most enticing ones as far as I was concerned—were dingy little places in dingy little streets, the walls and ceilings dark with smoke, the benches upholstered in the red cloth known as 'moleskin'. These were the cafés where men stopped for a coffee at seven in the morning on their way to work (although the coffee so soon after the War was concocted from roasted barley), where they played dominoes or draughts or cards in the evening and were given messages which had been left for them during the day and where towards the end of the week they borrowed a few francs from the owner.

Winter was the best time to be in the cafés. The terraces were glassed in and large wood-burning stoves created the sort of stifling atmosphere one needed and the condensation on the window somehow made you feel even warmer. There was a sort of malignant pleasure to be derived from seeing people outside hurrying through the sleet. Periodically the coffee machine emitted reassuring little jets of steam. There was a comforting racket—uninhibited but amiable arguments, cards being slammed triumphantly down on table-tops, dice rattling and the winner bellowing exultantly when he scored the all-conquering 421, the *patron* yelling at someone that he was wanted on the telephone. Chestnut-sellers would drift in and newspaper boys with *L'Intransigeant—L'Intran*, if you were a genuine Parisian—and *L'Aurore*. Cops and whores and factory hands mingled fraternally.

I got to know a good number of cafés and was happy in all of them but in the end I had to choose one particular one for my personal club: it wasn't done to spread oneself around. My café was mostly frequented by workers. They wore the same blue overalls that French workers had worn for generations together with the berets that before long were only to be seen on the heads of tourists. I was broke by this time and sufficiently scruffy to be admitted as a member of the guild. I never learnt to play *belote*, the universal card game, but that was overlooked when I proved myself an expert thrower of the dice. I made some good friends there. The *patron*'s wife used to sew an occasional button on my shirt and—this was the ultimate proof that I had been accepted—the *patron* would help me out with a small advance or let me run up a bill when things got too tough.

Already during that ride from the airport I had an unformed feeling that I would stay in France. There was no theory behind it, no solemn renunciation of my native land. Simply I was glad to be in France and couldn't imagine why I would want to leave. As weeks and then months went by I knew, again without making any solemn decision, that I never would leave.

I surmised that problems would arise but the only one to which I gave any thought was finding somewhere to live. Accommodation was in short supply like everything else. Some of the furnished rooms I occupied caused even my adoration of Paris to waver a bit. They were dark sepulchres furnished with great looming wardrobes which I never dared open for fear that a desiccated corpse might tumble out. Almost invariably a crucifix was pinned to the wall, presumably to discourage the vampires and werewolves who normally hung out there.

During a brief marriage, my wife and I lived in a crazy Left Bank hotel. I wrote about this fantastical establishment in a book which I published some years ago but since nobody read it there can't be any harm in repeating myself. It was a ramshackle place with a lift permanently stuck between two floors, with telephones which had apparently not worked since they had first been installed (a friend of mine used to summon his breakfast by blowing a powerful blast on a hunting horn), with doors which didn't lock and taps which didn't run, with a brass plate at the entrance arrogantly announcing that English was spoken when my wife and I were the only people in the place who spoke it.

The Florida was eccentric in plenty of other ways, in every way—the maddest box of tricks I ever came across. All the credit for the prevailing zaniness belonged to the proprietor. When we first met him, he struck us as a bit lugubrious. That was a mistaken impression if ever there was one. Before long we realised that Harlequin was lurking under that chapfallen exterior, only waiting for a chance to bound out and start dancing. Things that would have driven any other hotel proprietor out of his mind were just what Louis relished most. Whenever we inadvertently set fire to the curtains or broke a window, he was frankly delighted. Mishaps of the sort were clearly what he had been hankering after for years past to interrupt the monotony of existence. The lengthy periods when I was unable to pay the bill didn't worry him in the least. During such periods I not only failed to pay his bill, I borrowed money from him. He thought this reversal of normal procedure was hilarious. And on my birthday he presented me with a bottle of brandy.

Other Australians—writers and painters mostly—began to install themselves at the Florida. They were the sort of company Louis liked best. They were fellow-lunatics. Somebody came back one day with a collection of water pistols. Presumably Louis had had a deprived childhood; he had never seen water pistols before. He took to them enthusiastically. Ambushes were constantly being laid thereafter along the corridors and whether he was drenched or did the drenching Louis had the time of his life.

At fairly frequent intervals we would throw boisterous parties. You couldn't have kept Louis away from them—not that we would have dreamed of excluding him because he was more boisterous than anyone else. Wine spilt on the carpets, cigarette burns on the furniture and similar minor accidents made the hotel even more dilapidated than it had been before. Our cavortings eventually drove the staider guests in the place to go elsewhere. Louis was only too pleased to see the last of them although he didn't admit it. 'This used to be a respectable hotel,' he would say, trying hard to sound querulous. 'You've turned it into a madhouse.' But he couldn't conceal his pleasure at the transformation. He was much more at home in a madhouse than in a respectable hotel.

I would have happily stayed at the Florida for the rest of my life. I knew I would never find anything like it again. But there was Louis's wife. She was a cheerful old girl who was always ready to down a glass or two of wine with the rest of us. But she was not a madcap like Louis. He was too busy playing with water pistols to worry about the finances of the Florida. Berthe, on the other hand, fretted a good deal over the declining receipts. Decent bill-paying clients were increasingly rare. Those that did come never stayed long, not with water pistols being discharged along the corridors.

Berthe took over. Almost tearfully Louis announced one day that Berthe had determined to impose a more conventional existence on him. He was to be exiled as manager of a café on the outskirts of Paris. We tried to reason with him. Away from the Florida he would be lost, an orphan. What sort of fun could he expect with a lot of suburban clerks and shopkeepers as his only clients? What would he do without us? True, true, said Louis with emotion, but we would not desert him, surely. We would come to dine at his café *en famille*, no? As often as possible. Every day if we wanted.

That was all very well and we weren't shy about taking him up on the invitation to dine at his café. We had some memorable gatherings there although Berthe saw to it that no one carried a water pistol. Meantime, however, I had to look for alternative accommodation. I wasn't prepared to return to one of those ghoul-haunted furnished rooms and I knew I would never find a hotel as easygoing as Louis's Florida. The brief marriage had come to an end so that I didn't need an unduly extensive establishment. Not that I could have afforded it even if I had wanted to. I was writing a book which fortunately for the reading public was never finished. Nobody had shown any interest in giving me an advance on it. For the rest, I picked up a bit of money doing odd jobs. The owner of my chosen café hired me for a while to wash dishes in his minuscule kitchen and occasionally I had a night's work at the great central markets. My wages from these activities were enough, barely enough, to pay for something very modest indeed if I could find it.

In the end, I did. My new residence was modest all right. It was a sort of plywood cabin above a coal-shed in the courtyard of a big house in the rue Notre-Dame-des-Champs off the Boulevard Raspail. It was not merely modest, it was as austere as a monastic cell. My consolation was the concierge of the big house. She was of incredible antiquity and austere mien but I had got on the right side of her by offering to do her marketing one day when she was laid up with a cold in the head. From then on I was treated with extreme cordiality. I think I stood as high in her favour as the next-door concierge, her particular crony. Every so often she would invite me into her den to drink a glass of wine and would recount astonishing and frequently improper stories about different individuals who had lived in my shack or had had rooms in the big house.

Chatting with her on one occasion, she asked me what I did. She was barely literate but she was French and I knew my stocks would go up if I claimed to be a poet. A poet, was I? Ah, that explained why we got on so well together. She esteemed poets—they were a cut above the ordinary run of people. Years ago, another poet had lived there—not in my cabin but in a set of rooms in the house. Monsieur Poonde was his name. Perhaps I knew him?

Poonde? Poonde? No, I had never had the good fortune to meet the illustrious Poonde. Then it dawned on me. Pound, Ezra Pound! It was quite true that he had lived there. Not long ago in a book about the great man I saw a photograph of the courtyard—my courtyard—in the rue Notre-Dame-des-Champs. Nothing had changed. It was exactly as I was to know it twenty-five years later. The same plaster casts, left behind by some forgotten sculptor, were leaning against the wall.

'What sort of man was Monsieur Pound?'

'A very noisy gentleman . . .'

You ascended to my cabin by means of a stepladder. Inside, there was just enough space for the bed. Any visitors who might clamber up the ladder and open the door ran a risk of finding themselves tumbling into bed with me. It was too bad that no attractive young women ever came to call.

In the event, the only visitor I ever had was Pierre. Pierre was a taxidriver and I met him because he had entered a contest organised by some airline or other. The aim was to select the most typical representatives of various forms of transport— a London bus conductor, a Venetian gondolier, a Paris taxidriver. Pierre entered in the last of these categories.

One by one, candidates were brought before a jury and the same questions put to each. One question in particular was considered fundamental: 'You are driving around in your cab and you are simultaneously hailed by a ravishing young woman and a poor old lady with two heavy suitcases. Which of the two would you take?'

The contestants felt confident that they knew the answer to that one. The poor old lady, of course, with the two heavy suitcases. And why would that be their choice? Why, because it was only right to be kind to the elderly—one has a heart, *quoi*—what sort of a world would it be if one didn't spare a thought for the aged and infirm?

Pierre was ushered in. The same question was put to him and he gave the same answer as the other candidates. '*Pas d'hésitation*, the old biddy with the two heavy suitcases.'

'And why?'

'*Mon Dieu*, because there's an additional charge for suitcases, *voyons*.' He won.

The first prize was a free trip to Australia and someone from the Australian Embassy gave a cocktail party for Pierre on the eve of his departure. I don't know why I was invited. I know why I accepted. There would be things to eat. I found something better than cheese straws or canapés. Pierre. A tall fellow of about my own age he bore a striking facial resemblance to certain depictions of Richard III. He was dressed in irreproachable taste—perfectly pressed grey trousers, beautifully shined shoes, a blue blazer with brass buttons. He could have passed for one of the diplomats present. His manners were conspicuously good, his French was of unusual elegance. Such worldliness was almost intimidating but I thought I detected a sardonic glint in his eye.

When the party broke up Pierre for some reason asked whether he could drop me anywhere. 'If he was going towards Montparnasse . . .' He was. He made elaborate farewells and we went sedately downstairs together. I was still a little ill at ease in the presence of so much social aplomb.

Once in his taxi, Pierre was abruptly transformed. The refined upper-class diction made way for the characteristic drawl of the *titi*, the Parisian street boy. Dropping the ceremonious speech which was all I had heard so far from him, he addressed me in the familiar second person singular '*Eh, bien, mon vieux*, that was heavy going. I could see you weren't loving it, either. Let's go and drink some Calvados to get the taste of champagne out of our mouths.'

Before long, I came to understand that Pierre was a dual or rather a multiple personality. Depending on the circumstances, he could switch in an instant from the proletarian taxidriver to the urbane patrician I had met at the Embassy party and then as quickly back again with, moreover, innumerable variations in between. This ability to metamorphose himself enabled him to establish relationships with an extraordinary range of people. He had friends and acquaintances in every milieu imaginable. I was present when he discussed Céline with a well-known author, when he argued with another taxidriver about the innards of different engines, when he expounded the significance of an artist's paintings to the painter himself, when he gave some valuable advice on sexual peculiarities to a couple of tarts in a bar.

Whether or not the others learnt anything new, the two tarts undoubtedly picked up some useful hints. Sex was Pierre's speciality. He recounted uproarious stories of his amatory prowess which would have startled Kraft-Ebbing. Women, we were given to understand, staggered back unbelievingly on first sighting his sexual organ. 'Thirty-three centimetres!' Pierre would proclaim in reverent tones as though he himself was awed by such a phenomenon.

Once, as we sat on a café terrace, Pierre was moved to boast of his dimensions yet again. 'Thirty-three centimetres, Alister—can you imagine?' The waiter, an old friend, overheard the revelation. So did practically everyone else on the terrace: Pierre was not coy on the subject.

'*Allons, Monsieur Pierre*—thirty-three centimetres! It's not possible.'

'*Mon ami*,' said Pierre with deep gravity, 'I would be only too happy to provide ocular proof but I dare not. An inadvertent movement on my part and I might well put out one of your eyes.'

The trip to Australia which he had won left Pierre with only a hazy impression of my native land. I gathered that he and the bus conductor and the gondolier celebrated their triumph all the way there, throughout their stay and all the way back. I was touched to discover, however, that he had not forgotten me during his absence. He turned up one morning at the rue Notre-Dame-des-Champs and contemplated my cabin with commiseration.

'Let's have lunch together.'

'No money.'

'I can see that, *espèce d'imbécile*. Neither have I for the moment but I will have by lunchtime. Let's go over towards the Champs-Elysées—always plenty of passengers there. If they're Americans or English you can be my interpreter and your salary will be a decent meal. *Allons-y!*'

Thereafter, this was a more or less regular routine. Each morning I would take my place in the taxi beside Pierre and we would ply for hire. Towards noon, Pierre would count the takings. '*Bien, bien*, I think we can manage something a bit more succulent than we had yesterday.'

My talents as an interpreter were only rarely required. One day when we had picked up a middle-aged American couple, Pierre decided that it would be amusing if I were to pretend that I was French and had no more English than himself. The idea was that the Americans would talk together freely and that all sorts of scabrous remarks would be made which I would subsequently repeat to Pierre. Nothing in the least scabrous was said, to Pierre's disappointment. Meantime, the Americans were asking this and that. I interpreted and Pierre would make an effort to reply in his badly broken English. From time to time, I chipped in on my own account but since I had established myself as French, I was obliged to use an English as fragmentary as Pierre's and to assume a music hall French accent. When the Americans reached their destination, the woman gave judgment. 'Your friend,' she told Pierre, '*understands* English better than you do but you *speak* it much better than he does.' Pierre was ecstatic. 'Never forget,' he would say thereafter, 'that you may understand English better than I do but I'm the one who speaks it as it should be spoken.'

I was well aware that the amount of interpreting I had to do was a long way from compensating Pierre for the cost of my meals. Pierre promptly found a way of easing my conscience.

'Well, I'll tell you what. For a man of my distinction'—a derisive cackle of laughter at this point—'for a man of my distinction it's humiliating to have to curse drivers less skilled than myself, not to mention all those pedestrians with suicidal tendencies. Besides, the younger generation looks to me to set certain standards of behaviour. You have no reputation for gentility to preserve. I'll teach you the basic insults to be delivered and henceforward, when I give the signal, *you* do the cursing.'

I learnt some superbly foul language under Pierre's guidance and used it as instructed. 'Look at that cretin walking right against the lights,' Pierre would say, 'let him have it!' and I would let loose a spate of obscene invective.

George Orwell made it clear that he had greatly disliked being down and out in Paris. There were moments when I didn't much enjoy the experience myself. Thanks to Pierre and one or two others, though, I had a happier time of it than Orwell.

Chapter Two

I settled into the rabbit hutch on the rue Notre-Dame-des-Champs at the beginning of a murderously hard winter. An ill-favoured oil stove provided no comfort since I could not afford to buy oil for it. This may have been just as well. The hutch had no window nor any other ventilation and I would most probably have been asphyxiated. Most of the time I stayed in bed, fully clothed and with an overcoat and a tattered tablecloth to supplement the thin blankets.

But I had no regrets. Twinges of hunger were sometimes accompanied by twinges of self-pity but I was in Paris, my Paris, the great love of my life. That was all that mattered. Being poor in London, as I had been before coming to Paris, was no joke—Orwell would have got no argument from me on that point. You not only felt that passers-by would think it unseemly to notice if you fainted in the street but in addition you were also conscious of a pervasive moral disapproval. Lack of an adequate income in London was regarded as a sure indication of some fundamental flaw in one's character—not perhaps actually flagitious but nonetheless reprehensible.

You never had to feel guilty about your poverty in Paris. Nor did I. At the worst moments, I could walk confidently along the street with no thought that I should be ringing a bell and wailing, 'Unclean, unclean'. It was wealth—bourgeois wealth, in particular—which was regarded as unclean. Decent Parisians assumed—and were usually right—that only scoundrels became rich, politicians and people of that kind. Far from being considered suspicious, to be poor in Paris was a mark of respectability. It was nice to feel you were looked on with approval, even if you hadn't had a square meal for three days.

The vast Coupole brasserie was only a block away from the

rue Notre-Dame-des-Champs. Despite its imposing size and although it must have had a couple of thousand customers each day, it had something of the character of a neighbourhood café. There was nothing impersonal about it. Rather than one huge establishment, it was more like fifty or so small establishments housed in the same space. Every regular customer had his own few square yards. He wouldn't have dreamed of sitting at a table outside his chosen radius. The atmosphere was one of continual bustle but there was nothing hectic about it. You never felt that the waiters were waiting irritably to see you go. It had been a hang-out for artists and writers since its foundation in the early 1920s. The old bohemian atmosphere could still be inhaled there. Habitués were expected to dawdle. Nobody dawdled more consistently than I did.

Whenever I had managed to earn a few francs I would go to the Coupole as soon as it opened at six in the morning. I hadn't forgotten my personal café, the café I had adopted and that had adopted me, but it was on the other side of the city. In any case, it didn't have the same facilities. At the Coupole I could wash and shave in deliciously hot water— the only taps available to me in the rue Notre-Dame-des-Champs were in the courtyard and in winter frozen solid. For the price of a cup of coffee, I could sit in the Coupole for hours. The day's newspapers, rolled around wooden rods like Roman scrolls, were set out for the use of customers. I could read these or talk to the waiters (who themselves possessed a bohemian mentality) or scribble away at my impossible book—in those days, every café supplied paper and pen and ink on request.

The scribbling made me a figure of consequence. Nobody knew what I was writing or, for that matter, whether I could write at all (I had doubts myself periodically). But I wrote. That was enough. It made me the equal of Jean-Paul Sartre who used to squat toadlike in a corner where he received his admirers. It made me the equal of Samuel Beckett and Lawrence Durrell who also patronised the Coupole. It made me the equal of Genet, hardly more prepossessing than Sartre, and Jacques Laurent and the ex-convict Papillon. I was in distinguished company.

My great friend among the staff was one of the headwaiters, Monsieur Victor, who had held this position ever since the Coupole first opened. In his behaviour towards me, he mingled the esteem automatically extended in France to anyone claiming to be some sort of artist with a paternal benevolence. Sometimes he would slip me a surreptitious sandwich.

When I had made a bit more money than usual I would treat myself to a full-scale meal at the Coupole. Monsieur Victor would then take complete control. On these occasions he referred to himself, magisterially, in the third person.

'*Voilà ce que vous allez manger,*' he would say. 'A few oysters to begin with, I think. Yes, that would be best—half-a-dozen *claires*. Not *belons*. It doesn't matter whether you prefer *belons* or not. They have no character.'

'Well, I was actually thinking of some pâté, Monsieur Victor, or a slice or two of garlic sausage, perhaps.'

'Not another word! It is Victor who gives the orders, *n'est-ce pas*? And Victor tells you to eat a few oysters. Then a morsel of beef—Victor himself will select it. And a bottle of Chinon. *Ecoutez Victor.*'

In the end I always did.

Victor's successor was Monsieur Robert. He had saturnine, not to say satanic, features but he was as benign as Victor. By the time I came to know him I had found a job and was reasonably solvent but I usually managed to run out of money before pay day.

'Robert, I don't know if you've noticed it but we are getting towards the end of the month.'

'*En effet, cher ami, en effet*' and Robert would place his wallet on the table and go about his business. I would help myself and ten minutes later Robert would return, pick up his wallet and pocket it. He never looked to see what I had taken and he never asked me. Australian and English acquaintances brought up on the myth of the miserly French would gape unbelievingly at these transactions. They would ask whether the operation was a comedy put on for their benefit. It was not. It was Paris, my Paris.

The Coupole's clientèle was a bizarre conglomeration of types. First thing in the morning, most of the customers were as down at heel as I was and like me came along for the hot water and the newspapers. Towards lunchtime, you got a better class of people—writers and artists but prosperous ones, young businessmen talking with restrained excitement about advertising and manpower charts, politicians (nobody much cared for them), film producers and bank managers. These drifted away in the course of the afternoon and at about five o'clock were replaced by elderly ladies ('*Nos monuments historiques*', as Robert sardonically called them) wearing portentous hats and drinking tea.

None of the newspaper offices was situated in the vicinity but journalists crossed the city at all hours of the day or night to drink at the Coupole. I formed a lasting friendship with one of them. There was every reason why it shouldn't have lasted because Alain's brand of humour could frequently make one want to scramble for the nearest place of concealment.

Once when we were having what I had thought would be a quiet drink together he suddenly, without warning, began to upbraid me in shrill and disconcertingly audible tones.

'I've given you the best years of my life,' he screeched, 'I've given you tenderness, devotion—yes, and money, too, only you know how much! And now that you've taken everything from me, my heart, my youth, my little income, you desert me for that horrible, hateful Maurice! Oh, it's so cruel! How could you do it to me, how, how, how?'

By this time, he had an attentive audience of some five hundred people.

'I'll never forgive you, you hateful boy! Never, do you hear me?'

Like any other cocky twenty-five-year-old, I'd always imagined that I was indifferent to what the multitude might think of me. Alain rapidly convinced me that I was mistaken.

'Beast, beast, beast!' he screamed. Everybody in the place,

including the waiters, was following the scene with fascination.

'Listen, Alain, you son of a bitch. If you don't stop this bullshit I swear I'll walk out right now and leave you with the bill.'

'Maurice of all people! He's nothing but a little tart. Don't you realise that he's only after your money?'

'All right—I warned you.' Wincing under the concentrated gaze of the other customers, I got up and prepared to leave.

I had underestimated Alain. Grabbing my hand so that I was unable to pull away, he raised his voice several decibels and threw himself into his role with still more intensity. 'No, no, don't leave me, don't leave me! I'll kill myself if you desert me. I tell you I'll kill myself and I'll kill Maurice first. Have you no pity? Dear God, must it end like this?'

The suicide threat was attracting even more attention than the preceding performance. There was only one way to stop it. I sat down again. Alain at once resumed his wailing. 'Maurice! I wouldn't have believed it. If only it had been some other boy I wouldn't have minded so much. But Maurice!'

It was some time before I had the nerve to return to a place which I'd come to regard as my second, indeed my only, home.

The Coupole really became itself at night. I might have only enough for my usual cup of coffee but its long brightly lit glass façade was marvellously cheering. It loomed in the dark like a gigantic fun fair. I felt no rancour at the sight of customers gobbling up their meals. Quite the reverse. Somehow I had the sensation that I was eating just as well as they were. And once inside, there were invigorating smells from the kitchen and a convivial clinking of glasses, an irresistible animation. You might not have a franc in your pocket but it was impossible to be downcast in the Coupole.

It was at night that all the different categories of customer were jumbled together—the riff-raff to which I belonged, the businessmen, the film producers and the historical monuments and, like a parade of harlequins, the various crackpots and fantasts in which Paris then abounded.

At infrequent intervals these would include Raymond

Duncan, Isadora's fatuous brother. Piously 'Greek', he wore his hair down to his shoulder blades and was at all times clad in a robe woven for him by a group of dopey handmaidens who incomprehensibly allowed themselves to be exploited by him. He was a grotesque figure but his masquerade had been going on for so long that he had ceased to amuse anyone. We disdained him as an intruder. He had no recognised corner of his own. Indeed, he never sat down at all. When he paid one of his occasional visits, he would simply stalk around among the tables visibly and vainly craving attention and possibly hoping that someone would buy him a drink. I never saw anyone do so.

Monsieur de Beauharnais (nobody ever disputed his entitlement to this name) was a vastly different personage. He gave the impression of being permanently out of humour. Perhaps he was. He certainly did all he could to indicate that he would have been infinitely happier living under the First Empire. It might almost be said that he *was* living under the First Empire. His costume—top boots, frockcoat, fancy waistcoat and tall hat—was precisely what the well-dressed man was wearing in 1810. Cries of '*Vive l'Empereur!*' greeted his arrival in the Coupole. Monsieur de Beauharnais took these manifestations of imperial fervour as a perfectly normal civility which he acknowledged with a graceful nod to left and right. He would then sit down and extracting from his pocket a copy of *Le Moniteur* or some other paper of his preferred period would catch up on the latest news from the Austerlitz or Wagram front. You could tell how the Emperor's campaigns were progressing from the expression on Monsieur de Beauharnais's face as he read his paper. It was pitiful to see him during the retreat from Moscow.

I counted myself among Monsieur de Beauharnais's followers but I had a slight prejudice in favour of Ferdinand Lop, another of the mad wags to be seen most evenings at the Coupole. He was renowned as an indefatigable candidate for the presidency of the Republic. The only time I regretted that I was ineligible to vote in France was when I listened to Ferdinand Lop expounding his program at the Coupole. If elected, he proclaimed, he would at once initiate two major reforms: the suppression of all poverty after 10.00 pm (although, situated as I was, I would rather he had fixed the hour somewhat earlier) and the extension of the Boulevard St Michel to the coast.

Montparnasse and the Latin Quarter were about equally divided between intransigent followers of Lop—Lopistes, as they were known—and no less resolute opponents, the Antilopes. I was a thoroughgoing Lopiste. How could one fail to support the only man pledged to extend the Boulevard St Michel to the coast?

When more than ordinarily moved by Lop's discourses at the Coupole, we Lopistes spontaneously burst into the Lopiste hymn. It was sung to the tune of 'Jingle Bells' and the words left no doubt whatever as to our sentiments:

'Lop, Lop, Lop,
Lop, Lop, Lop,
Lop, Lop, Lop, Lop, Lop,
Lop, Lop, Lop,
Lop, Lop, Lop,
Lop, Lop, Lop, Lop, Lop . . . '

The Antilopes held that the Master (as he was always addressed) was not merely on the wrong track but that his motives were wholly evil. As he discoursed to his disciples in the Coupole, the Antilopes would interrupt with vociferous charges that he was a hireling of the Communist Party, that he was in the pay of the banking interests, that he was planning to take over the Latin Quarter by armed force, that if elected he would introduce Triple and perhaps Quadruple Summer Time. Everyone knew, they would clamour, while the Lopistes shook outraged fists at them, that poverty should not be suppressed until 11.00 pm at the earliest and that it was the Boulevard St Germain rather than the Boulevard St Michel which should be extended to the coast. '*A bas Lop*! Down with the Boulevard St Michel!'

At the meetings periodically convened by Lop to clarify his theories (as if they needed any clarification), Lopistes and Antilopes bawled impassioned insults at each other. I was present at one especially violent gathering. Lop concluded his speech ('Yes, ladies and gentlemen, to the coast, I say!') and invited the audience, university students most of them, to put any questions they might wish. A young man rose to his feet and spoke with undisguised emotion. 'For years,' he said, 'I have been a Lopiste, unswerving in my loyalty to the Master. Recently, however, I was shown a photograph of undeniable authenticity which has caused me to revise my position radically. This photograph, my friends, taken during the war, showed the interior of a German submarine. And those present in that submarine consisted of Hitler, Göring, Goebbels—and Ferdinand Lop! I accuse Ferdinand Lop of having master-minded the U-boat campaign!'

'A vile falsehood, a calumny!' bellowed Lop. 'At no time did I respond to the approaches made to me by Hitler and his associates. The photograph in question can only be a montage concocted by my enemies. De Gaulle? Churchill? A certain waiter at the Coupole known to all of you for his anti-Lop sentiments? It is for you to discover the ruffian responsible.'

The meeting, as they say, broke up in disorder. To cries of 'Lop, the war criminal!' from the Antilopes, the Lopistes responded with a sacramental rendition of the Lopiste hymn:

'Lop, Lop, Lop,
Lop, Lop, Lop,
Lop, Lop, Lop, Lop, Lop . . .'

With half humanity cringing in case some nitwitted sopho-more should accuse them of a breach of political correctness, it seems almost incredible that there was a time when students were able to take life light-heartedly. They could, though, and they did. There must be a large number of lawyers and notaries and surgeons who remember Ferdinand Lop with gratitude as an unfailing begetter of laughter.

What I found peculiarly appealing about all the nonsense of Monsieur de Beauharnais and Ferdinand Lop was that nobody ever jeered at them. Both were treated with respect—mock respect, of course, but with no mockery apparent. But was Lop, in particular, as barmy as he appeared? Or was he diverting himself by seeing how far he could carry absurdity without cracking our courteous deference?

The possibility first crossed my mind one evening when Pierre and I were drinking at the Coupole. The Master joined us at our table. 'This is in the strictest confidence,' he told us with deep solemnity, 'but I know I can count on your discretion.' He looked around to make sure nobody was eavesdropping. 'My engagement to Princess Margaret has definitely been broken off.'

Pierre, always equal to any occasion, adopted an expression in which incredulity and perturbation were impeccably blended. 'But, *Maître*, surely this can be no more than a regrettable lovers' tiff. With so much depending on the marriage . . .'

'No, *mon cher*,' Lop replied. 'Our Government has informed me that in no circumstances can it countenance the match.'

'Incredible, *Maître*! What inconceivable short-sightedness! These politicians! Can they not see what such a union would do to cement relations between England and France?'

Lop smiled wearily. 'Of course, of course, *mon cher*. But you overlook a fundamental difficulty. Were I to enter into marriage with Her Royal Highness I would be compelled to take up residence at Buckingham Palace. The Government cannot agree to my leaving France at this critical time.'

In the intervals between saluting Monsieur de Beauharnais and listening to Ferdinand Lop's closely reasoned arguments in favour of extending the Boulevard St Michel, we could always cluster round the Coupole's resident scholar. We never knew his name. To reveal it, he explained, would place him in mortal danger. As the repository of certain vital secrets, he was being sought by the intelligence services of half-a-dozen powers. The fiends would stop at nothing to prevent him from telling all he knew. We could call him Monsieur X.

If he didn't tell us all he knew, he told us enough to demonstrate that he was a man of prodigious erudition. Science, literature, history—he was at home in every field of human knowledge and we learnt things we had never suspected. Constantinople, for instance—none of us had realised until Monsieur X threw out the information that Constantinople was a mediaeval poet, unduly neglected but whose compositions were on a par with those of Vercingetorix. We hadn't known that Newton's Fourth Law was embodied in British jurisprudence and that it stipulated the penalties for house-breaking and counterfeiting. Hieroglyphs, Monsieur X explained to one of his listeners, were only dangerous in the mating season and were at all times notably less aggressive than cosines.

We were so awed by Monsieur X's scholarship that it came as no surprise to us when he obtained an appointment as a high-school teacher. A newspaper report which appeared not long afterwards shattered us all. Monsieur X, it stated, had been arrested and sentenced to a prison term for having used forged papers to get the post. At least that was the official story. Our own view was that one of the intelligence services must have caught up with him at last.

For me, there was no other place quite like the Coupole. The Dôme was never so welcoming. However hard you tried (supposing you wanted to try) there was no hope of summoning up the ghosts of Hemingway and his friends. The Select, across the road, was brisk, too brisk to make a suitable setting for Monsieur de Beauharnais and Ferdinand Lop. A few hundred metres away was the Closerie des Lilas. Little brass plates were fixed to certain tables bearing the names of celebrated clients who had sat there. Lenin was one of them. It was unlikely that he would have chosen to infest the Closerie in its present guise. The decor was refined. The clientele was well dressed, well behaved and well heeled. Lenin would no longer have felt at home there and the prices would be well out of his reach. They were certainly out of mine.

If you went outside Montparnasse (but habitués like myself

didn't often do anything so bizarre) you could choose between the St Germain cafés. I was quite happy to leave the choosing to other people. The Deux Magots (or was it the Flore?) was full of tourists, when these started coming back to Paris, all looking for some existentialists to make an appearance. Lipp specialised in serving politicians. Unless you had spent some years making a public pest of yourself as a minister or deputy (and collecting a fortune in the process) you were made to feel an intruder.

But there was never a moment when your heart wasn't lightened by the prospect of dropping in at the Coupole to shake hands with the waiters, all of them old friends, to listen to Robert's ironic reflections on life and the vagaries of customers, to eat a couple of sausages with fried potatoes (the cheapest dish on the menu and no less delicious for that) and to drink a *sérieux* of beer. (If someone else was paying, you ordered a *formidable* instead.) The Coupole was more precious to us than the Louvre. And we didn't *have* to look at Sartre in his corner.

CHAPTER THREE

For this reason and that, I had to vacate the rue Notre-Dame-des-Champs. The concierge brought out a bottle of wine and, after we had emptied it, bade me a lachrymose farewell. 'Ah, if only all poets were like you! Monsieur Poonde was well enough in his way but he never offered to do the marketing for me.'

I was one up on Ezra Pound.

The next few weeks brought me as close as I ever came to sympathising with George Orwell's disconsolate reaction to the experience of poverty in Paris. I had no work, no money, nowhere to live—and it was still winter. I don't suppose it really rained round the clock but that is how it seems in retrospect. The temperature was subzero.

Given my insouciant (feckless?) behaviour since I arrived in Paris, I might have foreseen that some such situation would inevitably arise sooner or later and have made arrangements to meet it. On the boat coming from Australia, I had sometimes speculated as to what might lie ahead, more and more often and with increasing agitation as we drew closer to our destination. A friend had lent me a hundred pounds before I sailed. That was quite a lot of money then but I had nonetheless managed to spend most of it in Bombay, our solitary port of call. I would be arriving in Europe with practically nothing in my pocket, with a circle of friends and acquaintances consisting of just two compatriots who had beaten me to it, and with no means of running home if the worst came to the worst. Which I felt confident it would.

I felt it might help if I knew that at least one or two of the artists and writers among my fellow passengers were, so to speak, in the same boat. I questioned them. They were reassuring. Why, they themselves had been as foolhardy as I had, they told me merrily. Like myself, they had no money—perhaps a thousand pounds but certainly no more. They didn't know where they were going to stay, either—after leaving Cousin Maud's or Uncle George's, that is. Of course they had their return tickets—that was plain commonsense. Somehow their idea of light-hearted recklessness didn't do much to comfort me.

In the joy of falling in love with Paris, I had not given any further thought to such minor problems as staying alive. And, on the whole, things hadn't worked out too badly. I had earned some money here and there and apart from my dishwashing, Alain had passed me an occasional job of translating. Thanks to Louis's unorthodox approach to hotel keeping, I had been reasonably comfortable for some months. Pierre's meals had come in very useful. The Coupole had offered an incomparable refuge.

But now? Out in the cold, no immediate solution occurred to me. Nor any more distant solution, if it came to that. I had a remarkable lack of qualifications for any job. I disliked the idea of battening on Pierre and whatever other friends I had made. It was permissible to sit in the Coupole over a single cup of coffee but I could hardly install myself there without ordering even that.

From time to time during the destitute existence I was now leading, I would decide that I had conceded enough to my middle-class upbringing. Uninvited, I would turn up at the tiny flat which Alain occupied with his wife Michelle and their small daughter Noëlle. They charitably insisted that I was welcome although I knew perfectly well that, on the contrary, I was an intolerable nuisance. But, nuisance or not, I would eat and drink more than my fair share of whatever was available. After dinner, I would be told to make myself as comfortable as was possible on the floor under the living room table. Quite often I did.

Quite often I didn't. Then I would tramp the streets all night. I didn't like it much. Nights can be long. Draping that particular phase of my existence in an illusory glamour would be as silly as snivelling over it. During these nocturnal jaunts, I devised an antidote to my self-inflicted misery, imagining myself as a character in a romantic novel or as a sort of Chatterton (although he at least had his garret) or as a Rimbaud, the *poète maudit*. Flinging myself in the Seine was another scene which I enacted for my own benefit. This particular daydream saw to it that I was fished out by the crew of a passing yacht. The owner was a ravishing millionairess. She herself nursed the young poet back to health. Thereafter things developed in strict accordance with the laws of the romantic novels. Sometimes, however, the story had a sad ending. I drowned and everyone was remorseful at not having been nicer to me while they had the chance. These visions were soothing for as long as they lasted but they didn't last long. Self-dramatisation was a poor substitute for a good meal. More and more, my reveries were of food, piled high and smoking. Usually, I don't know why, the image was of *choucroute, choucroute* with at least three varieties of sausages. When I got tired of *choucroute* I would switch to *cassoulet*, steaming kidney beans and plenty of Toulouse sausage and great chunks of goose. And of course a *formidable* of beer—not a *sérieux*, a *formidable*. In my imagination I ate some tremendous meals at that time. I don't think I've ever eaten so heartily since.

By and large I wasn't too depressed. There was just one crisis. That was when on one especially wet night I became dismally conscious of water squelching through the soles of my shoes. I should have been used to it by then but I wasn't. For some reason, the squelching suddenly struck me as unspeakably tragic. I turned into a doorway and had a good cry about it. After that I felt a little better but only a little. I was deeply and sincerely sorry for myself.

Love apparently really does conquer all. I was still in love with my city. Somehow it was more satisfactory to lean over a bridge and stare gloomily down at the Seine than to stare at the Thames, let alone the Yarra. Telling oneself that one was at least trudging along the Quai Voltaire rather than Collins Street or the Strand made one feel better—made me feel better, at any rate. And humiliating as the confession may be, it's not altogether impossible that I had some murky notion that the experience would make a pathetic chapter should I ever write my memoirs. That, I now realise, was remarkably far-seeing on my part . . .

Some richly enjoyable encounters took place. I got to know three or four *clochards*, the permanent down-and-outs of Paris. According to Parisian folklore, there were former doctors and lawyers and professors among the *clochards*, rebels who had disdainfully rejected bourgeois society and their role in it. I kept hoping to meet some of these picturesque outcasts but, if they existed at all, I never came across them. None of my *clochards* showed any inclination to discuss corporate law or to produce an apposite quotation from the classics. Indeed, they were disinclined to talk much at all. However, once they had understood that I was not a journalist in search of copy or a disguised missionary come to save their souls, they allowed me to join in such spasmodic conversation as did take place. Five or ten minutes would pass in silence while a bottle of notably disgusting wine went from hand to hand. Their tolerance for alcohol was not high. It took only a few gulps of whatever was offering to inflame them. Then someone would start things going by making a comment on the politicians currently mismanaging the nation. The company was at once invigorated. They execrated all politicians from extreme left to extreme right. In particular, they loathed the sort of politician who, pocketing his salary and anything else which might be to hand, specialised in weeping over the 'dispossessed' or 'underprivileged' classes. That was a conversation I could join in with unaffected enthusiasm so we got along very well. My *clochards* taught me that rage was a much more satisfactory emotion than gloom.

They gave me some other useful lessons, too. Sleeping out of doors in the daytime was not to be recommended, they explained; you were likely to be harassed by any cop who happened to pass by. For the same reason, you should always have some money on you—I think the sum required was fifty francs. So long as you could produce a note for that amount, you could not be arrested for vagrancy. And it was undesirable to be a vagrant: you were hauled off to the cells and next morning stripped and scrubbed down with carbolic. Most *clochards* had the requisite note sewn into the lining of their coats. It was inviolate, not to be spent even when things were at their worst. Better to go hungry and thirsty than to be scrubbed with carbolic.

I was taken along to certain restaurants where, at closing time, the proprietor would distribute the leftovers. They were often quite succulent. Each of these benevolent establishments had its regular quota of *clochards*. It was unheard-of for one group to intrude on another group's territory. I was fortunate to be put up for membership, so to speak, of my friends' personal restaurants.

Briefer but notably more outlandish than my association with the *clochards* was my meeting with Laure. As usual, it was raining. Somehow or other, I had a couple of francs in my pocket, enough to buy a beer or a glass of wine. But it would have been stupid to give myself this treat too soon. I made up my mind to wait until I had had all the drenching I could endure. That would be the moment to go to a café and get warm.

I held off until about 4.00 am. There was only one other customer in the café. She was an attractive young woman but I was too wet, too cold and too hungry to be bothered ogling her. Nobody ever drank a glass of wine as slowly as I did. The proprietor gave no sign of resentment but at six o'clock he announced that he was closing up. The young woman went out first. Unlike me, she had not had to make do with a solitary drink and was distinctly wobbly. Twice, as she crossed the boulevard, she almost wobbled under a car. On the whole, I didn't give a damn whether she lived or died but I thought I might as well save her life since I had nothing else to do. Catching up with her, I initiated an absurd boy scout dialogue. 'Excuse me, Madame, but you don't seem very well. Can I be of any assistance?'

I was quite prepared to be told to go to hell and would have been quite happy to do so. After eyeing me for a second or two, she apparently concluded that I was not attempting a seduction. She was quite right.

'You're very kind. Well, you can see for yourself, I've had too much to drink. I'm not sure I can get home by myself. If you could help me . . .'

'Gladly.'

She was lucky to have met with someone as chivalrous as me. Her room was only a couple of hundred yards away, it turned out, but she would never have made it without my assistance. On the sixth floor. No lift. I practically had to carry her upstairs.

Arrived at her doorway, she thanked me with surprising coherency and added the civil hope that she had not taken me too far from my own home. This was an opportunity for histrionics that was too good to miss.

'Please don't worry about that. I have no home.'

'You mean you're tramping the streets in this weather?'

'I'm afraid so. Goodnight.'

Once again, she took a good look at me. Then, 'I don't think you'll jump to any conclusions. I'm far too drunk to be interested in what you might be thinking and you look far too ill to be thinking it anyway. There's only one room and one bed. If you want to sleep here tonight . . .'

The melodramatic role I had adopted should have led me to refuse. But—a bed! I protested for perhaps thirty seconds. Then we went in, got undressed, went to bed and, immediately, both of us, fell asleep.

We woke late. Both of us were quite naked. Sitting up beside my hostess, I shook her hand. Hands are shaken with monotonous frequency in France but it is unlikely that any hand was ever shaken in such unusual circumstances.

'Good morning, Madame. I hope you slept well.'

'Very well indeed, thank you, Monsieur. And you?'

'Wonderfully well. And really I don't know how to thank you for your hospitality.'

'On the contrary, Monsieur, it is I who must thank you for your kindness last night.'

Neither of us saw the comedy of a man and a woman, naked in bed together, exchanging civilities as though we were at a polite dinner party. The young woman demurely averted her eyes as I got up and dressed. We said goodbye and I never saw her again.

All my relationships at this time—not that there were many of them—were equally platonic. Monique, for instance. She turned up at Alain's flat one night when I had once again waived my principles and gone there to scrounge a meal. She was pretty in a boyish sort of way. Her attire was boyish, too, not to say virile—slacks, a rolltop sweater and a cloth cap. She was full of a joyous vitality which immediately attracted me as it must have attracted everyone who met her. With a substantial meal and plenty of wine inside me, I stopped being the tragic waif and laughed wholeheartedly at Monique's jests. I actually managed to make her laugh—no great feat because she laughed easily. We got along very well. So well that, on hearing my sad story, she came up with a suggestion.

'Look, I've got a flat in Montmartre—it's my uncle's but he lives in the country and never comes to Paris. Why don't you come and stay there?'

Nobody else could have created a relationship so rapidly which made any 'Oh, I couldn't possibly impose myself' completely ridiculous.

'That sounds wonderful.'

'Wait till you see it. You may prefer a Salvation Army hostel. Besides, there's another detail which mustn't be overlooked. It must have crossed even your innocent little Australian mind that I'm a lesbian.'

'I'd never have guessed.'

'Like hell! Anyway, a roof over your head is all I'm offering, *d'accord*?'

'*D'accord*.'

Monique's uncle's flat was a huge cavernous place such as only the French bourgeoisie could bear to inhabit. I remember it as having about seventeen rooms although I suppose there can't really have been so many. What is quite certain is that not one of them had the smallest item of furniture, nothing, not a table, not a chair, not a bookcase, not a wardrobe. Unbeknownst to Uncle, Monique (but she preferred to be called Nick) had sold the lot. Evidently there had been no takers for the kitchen stove which was the only object still in place. Its function, however, was purely decorative: the gas had long since been cut off because of unpaid bills. Callers unfamiliar with the domestic arrangements—usually duns—stabbed at the doorbell in vain: the electricity had been cut off, too. So had the water. There were two mattresses in adjoining rooms. At night, we groped our way to them with candle stubs dripping grease over the floor.

During the day, Nick worked in a record shop. That made sense. It enabled us to survive. My own contribution consisted of scribbling away with fatuous optimism at my wretched, unprofitable book. By five o'clock in the afternoon it was dark. Then there was nothing to do except lie on my mattress and stare at the ceiling until Nick came home. She had generally managed to steal a small sum from the till so that we could eat some bread and cheese or a bit of sausage most nights. Quite often, one or another of her lesbian pals would arrive with a bottle of something and a Camembert or a wedge of Brie. We didn't do so badly. And, hungry or not, we never once lapsed into depression. Left to myself I might have succumbed but it was inconceivable with Nick around. She had enough vitality for the two of us.

Friday night was special. That was payday. Nick would come galloping in and as soon as I heard her at the door, I was off the mattress and slavering. 'What have we got to eat?'

'Ham and tomatoes and bread and two slices of cooked beef and two bottles of *rouge*—what the hell else do you want?'

'Cigarettes, unless you want to see me dead at your feet' (going without cigarettes was the hardest thing to put up with).

'Of course I've got cigarettes, you bloody fool. And I

managed to snitch a packet of butter from a stall on the way home.'

Those were delicious meals we had, squatting in the darkness of the empty flat. We would stuff ourselves unashamedly, wiping our plates clean with the last of the bread. We would belch contentedly and light our cigarettes—the first perhaps for forty-eight hours during which we had suffered appalling pangs. Drawing the smoke deep into our lungs and holding it there for minutes at a time was the height of voluptuousness. Cancer was the least of our worries. Then we would go out to see what was happening in Montmartre.

There was always something happening in that raucous, disreputable district—fire-eaters and sword-swallowers would perform on the footpaths, drunken old girls would be singing bawdy songs in the cafés, street vendors would be selling rickety objects to the tourists, touts would be furtively inviting passers-by to come and watch a pornographic film and cops would bestir themselves when they felt like it, grab some old customer and hustle him into the waiting van. Nick and I came to know them all and to drink with them all—the sword-swallowers, the ancient drunks, the touts, the ubiquitous whores, even the cops. We would amble from café to café, in between whiles pausing at one of the stalls where pungent *chorizo* sausages were sizzled over a charcoal fire while you waited. They were smeared with an incandescent sauce and we normally succeeded in eating three or four of them in spite of what we had just gobbled at home.

'Ah, that's the stuff to put blood in your veins,' the stall-keeper would tell me and, affecting not to notice Nick's obvious sexual disposition, 'with the stamina you'll get from that sauce you'll be able to keep Madame happy all night.' 'Just try it,' Nick would snarl at me.

We learnt a lot in the course of these Friday night outings. One of the whores proposed to introduce Nick to a lesbian brothel where she could earn infinitely more than the record shop was prepared to pay. I pleaded with her to accept. 'For God's sake, Nick, you'd be combining business and pleasure.

35

Think of all the food we could buy. And the wine. And the cigarettes. And I could be your pimp. You won't mind me beating you up when you don't bring enough money home?'

Nick thought it over but finally declined. I was never to be a pimp. I did consider going in for a little light larceny. A professional pickpocket with whom we occasionally drank gave me a crash course in his art. He was forced to recognise, however, that I showed no aptitude. 'You'd better go in for something like smash-and-grab,' he told me commiseratingly, 'something that doesn't need any finesse.'

Not everyone in Montmartre was as convivial. Once Nick and I were bailed up by some very disagreeable-looking thugs. They would appreciate it, they said, if we were to hand over whatever we might have in our pockets. After which, they would be delighted to give the lady an unforgettable hour or two of their company. I considered making a run for it but there seemed every reason to suppose that the thugs could run faster than I could. Also, I felt I owed it to Nick to put up at least a token resistance. Livid with unmanly terror, I got ready to lash out. My efforts in that direction would have been as maladroit as my attempts to practise pickpocketing. I only hoped that I might be allowed to live.

I needn't have worried. Nick's charming features were transformed into the likeness of a Tibetan devil-mask. A flick-knife of awesome dimensions miraculously appeared in her hand. In a low vicious voice she announced what she could do with it and would like to do with it. Our aggressors hesitated. With Nick's blade weaving in front of them, they didn't hesitate for long. 'Just as well for them,' I told Nick as they backed off, 'another minute and, take it from me, I would have let them have it.'

'Like hell.'

By the time it began to get light, we would have spent Nick's wages to the last centime. Refreshed, we would stumble back to the great empty bourgeois apartment. We still had enough cigarettes to keep us going for a day or so . . .

Those penurious months in Montmartre were among the

happiest I ever spent. Just being indoors was wonderful. I couldn't have enjoyed myself more if I'd been living in the Ritz—certainly a good deal less. With Nick, I laughed as I have not often laughed since. I seem to remember that we were more or less constantly rolling about with amusement over everything that happened or didn't happen. I looked forward to Friday night as my betters looked forward to the Marquis de Cuevas's next masked ball, if indeed they did look forward to it. Camembert and *chorizos* never tasted so good again. I loved Nick from my heart and I do still now that she is dead— all her generosity and courage, her gaiety and marvellous response to life obliterated in a stupid motor accident.

CHAPTER FOUR

Against all the odds, I found a job. Nick received the news with cries of distress. She had a natural affinity with anyone of dubious social standing. Drop-outs, voluntary or involuntary, were her speciality. To see me teetering on the edge of respectability appalled her. 'You've got a job? A job—*you*! I suppose you won't want to know me in future. Can I come and peer at you through the window while you're dictating to your secretary? You in a job! God! Maybe I should have let you become my pimp after all.'

'Of course, you should. However, it's too late now. If you hadn't been so damned prudish you would have saved me from leading an upright, god-fearing life. It's all your fault. Don't blame me if I end up with a wife and four children and a lawnmower.'

The job was with some American organisation. American organisations were all over Paris in those days. They were known by initials—USSFA, USPDQ, USNBG. In some way I can't remember I'd heard that USCAD or USRAT was looking for someone who could write a more or less literate sentence. I thought I could manage that. I submitted my candidature and was summoned to an interview. I went along without much hope. My bedraggled appearance, I felt sure, would not help. Nor would my straggly hair. Not to mention my clothes which looked as if they had come from a rubbish bin. One or two items had.

I was received by an amiable fellow who winced a bit at the sight of me—which was what I'd anticipated—but who gave no sign that I might as well turn right round and go away. He seemed satisfied with my answers to his catechism. The job, he told me, was mine. Subject, of course, to what he bewilderingly called a 'favourable advisory determination'. He had me there. Seeing my puzzlement, he obligingly translated the expression. It meant that the American security services would determine whether or not I was in the pay of the Kremlin. This proviso didn't perturb me in the least. A regular income, I told myself exultantly, was imminent. It wouldn't be long now before I could start in on the *choucroute* and *cassoulet*. My political activity had never consisted of anything worse than blanketing all politicians with a comprehensive anathema. There was no trace of communism in *my* past.

Not all my acquaintances could claim as much. Sam, for example, was now the lavishly paid Paris correspondent of an English newspaper, on chummy terms with everyone of any social, financial or other distinction. In spite of which I was ready to bet that *he* would never have got a favourable advisory determination from the investigators. Back in the 1930s he had been a card-carrying and (so it was widely believed) bomb-carrying communist. In his student days at Melbourne University he had been set on by a bunch of stalwart patriots and thrown in the lake. These scandalous facts had not been forgotten. A fat chance he would have had of working for USRAT or whatever it was called.

His headquarters was the bar of the exceedingly chic Crillon Hotel where he spent most of the day and sometimes a sizeable part of the night. There he would collect bowerbird scraps from which he wove his daily gossip column. Ordinarily I wouldn't have dared to enter such a superior place and, given my present ruffianly aspect, it was even less appropriate that I should do so. But it was only a hundred metres along the boulevard from where I had been interviewed and I thought Sam might perhaps buy me a drink to celebrate my forthcoming employment.

I marched in trying to look like an eccentric duke. Sam obligingly ordered a drink for me and I was about to tell him my news (not that I expected it to get a mention in his column) when the American who had just promised me the job came into the bar. Naturally, Sam knew him—he knew everybody. 'Hi, Fred,' he said genially, 'come and have a drink' and, indicating me, 'Do you know Alister Kershaw—the shrewdest undercover man we ever had in the Party?'

There goes my favourable advisory determination, I thought in a spasm of anguish, there goes the job and the income and the *choucroute* and the *cassoulet*. Nick would be delighted, no doubt, but much as I loved her that was not enough to console me. Back to the unlit, unfurnished, gasless, unelectrified flat, the mattress on the floor—after coming so close to solvency it was hard to contemplate.

'Jesus, Sam! Will you please explain that you're just joking?'

Sam liked his joke. He had no intention of letting it go. 'Oh, I don't want to exaggerate, Fred. Alister wasn't in the top bracket. But he provided some useful information now and again. He earned his roubles.'

'Please, Sam, *please*!'

'Those details of Australia's coastal defences—they certainly were pleased about that in Moscow, I can tell you!' I felt like putting my head down on the bar and sobbing my heart out.

The American proved to have a mild sense of humour. He took Sam's quip as no more than that. In due course I was favourably determined and got the job. It had been a terrible moment, though.

With money to spare (the Americans paid generously) I was able to see a Paris very different from the one I was used to. Hobnobbing with *clochards* should have given me a virtuous distaste for the sybaritic life. It didn't. I enjoyed the unfamiliar luxuries without a pang. The first of these consisted of installing myself grandly in the 'best' quarter of Paris, the sixteenth *arrondissement*.

I was one of nature's proletarians, never really at home in the sixteenth. For one thing I couldn't get used to the obsequious attitude of the shopkeepers. In Montparnasse and Montmartre, I had been greeted with, '*Alors, Alister*, veal (or cauliflower or salami or cod or whatever it might be) is cheap today. Come on, take a pound and I'll buy you a drink. Well, if you're broke, you can pay later . . .' That wasn't the style in my new district. 'Ah, Monsieur Kershaw, how charming of you to drop in. I can recommend the foie gras today. A gentleman with your impeccable taste will undoubtedly appreciate its exceptional quality . . .'

Although USRAT paid me handsomely, I somehow still managed to run short more or less regularly. Obsequious they might be but the shopkeepers of the sixteenth were not as easy-going in the matter of payment as those I'd hitherto been accustomed to. There was just one very superior joint frequented by the gentry where it was customary to settle the bill at the end of the month. This accordingly was the shop I was periodically compelled to deal with. Unfortunately, it stocked nothing but the most luxurious tidbits. Whenever I was unable to buy a loaf of bread and a bit of cheese for ready money, I would perforce ring this establishment and ask that some caviar and foie gras be delivered. 'Oh, and by the way,' I would add negligently, 'you might have your boy pick up a couple of packets of cigarettes at the same time.' My friends came to realise that when I served caviar and vintage champagne, that meant that I hadn't a centime in my pocket.

Most of the other occupants in my block of flats had titles, whether bogus or not I never knew. We would bow austerely if we happened to pass each other in the hall but, with one exception, that was as far as it went. The one exception had a genuine title and an illustrious one at that. We met while collecting our mail from the concierge's lodge. The book I was carrying attracted his attention. He had read it and made some remark about it which struck me as extremely perceptive. We chatted for a while about books and when we parted he said amiably that he hoped he would have the pleasure of seeing me again. I said I hoped so, too. He absent-mindedly omitted to tell me his name.

Some weeks later the telephone rang. 'Monsieur Kershaw? This is Maximilien de – – – ,' one of the great names of France. 'I was wondering if by any chance you would be free to dine next Thursday?'

One of my facetious friends, of course, having a little fun. Alain? Pierre? 'Well, I'll have to look up my engagement book.

Next week as it happens I'm rather more than ordinarily busy.'

There was a moment's silence at the other end of the line. 'Of course, I quite understand. Still my wife and I would be so pleased . . .'

'Yes, yes, yes, yes, but I can't accommodate every Tom, Dick and Harry who wants to see me. Monday I've promised to look in on the Perpetual Secretary of the French Academy, Tuesday I've got to face that wretched old duchess, Wednesday the President . . .'

A longer pause followed. 'Perhaps the week after? I was so interested in what you had to say about Céline.'

Abruptly and horrifyingly I remembered the conversation I had had with my neighbour. Once, in Australia, I had made a similar *gaffe*. This was much worse. I proffered stumbling excuses and incoherent explanations. The Count, when he finally understood the cause of my absurd performance, thought it was hilarious. We dined together, we got on very well and I saw quite a lot of him and his charming wife thereafter.

But dining with the upper classes was not the only change in my way of life. Although I naturally remained faithful to the Coupole I felt no remorse when I gave preference to the Grand Véfour, the most attractive restaurant in the world and, with the great Raymond Oliver presiding over the kitchens, one of the most gastronomically rewarding. Jean Cocteau (who had designed the ashtrays) was often there. His presence, like that of Colette, another regular visitor, gave me the sensation that I, too, was part of the smart social-artistic world. The only drawback was that the synthetic proletarian Jean-Paul Sartre also sneaked in from time to time.

On sunny afternoons I would leave my USRAT colleagues to get on with the drudgery while I took a chauffeur-driven limousine to the Bois de Boulogne and drank champagne cocktails on the terrace of the Cascade. With Australia's gruesome trains fairly fresh in my memory, it was an especially voluptuous pleasure to go to the Gare de Lyon and take one of the incomparable luxury trains to the South of France for the weekend. I bought my aftershave lotion from the most expensive *parfumerie* on the rue St-Honoré.

Part of my salary was paid in dollars which, with the franc liable to unpredictable fainting fits, met with no objection from me. This arrangement led to my discovery that I was endowed with an astonishing gift. I had always known that I was not equipped to attract money, but I had not before realised that I had a unique talent for repulsing it. So soon after the war nobody changed dollars at a bank. You went to a black-market dealer who offered significantly better rates. I allowed my dollars to accumulate and when it became imperative to make use of them called on my dealer (we each had our own preferred operator), handed over a thin bundle of dollars and received in return a thick bundle of francs. The first time I did so, the franc was immediately devalued. If I had only waited twenty-four hours I would have got more from a straightforward exchange at the bank than I had got from my dealer.

Undeterred, I allowed my dollars to accumulate once again. Once again I called on my dealer. Once again the franc was promptly devalued. Shortly afterwards, I had confirmation that it was no coincidence, that I really did exercise a sort of upside-down power over the country's economy. The price of gold had been steadily rising for six months. One of my colleagues announced that he was going out to buy some gold coins. It's just as well, I told him, that I don't have any—if I did, the price of gold would drop overnight. 'You,' he said with unaccountable irritation, 'are totally paranoiac. And I'll prove it. I'll give you one of my coins, the price will go up again and that'll put an end to your idiotic theory.' He was a nice fellow and I hated to see him heading for disaster. There was no reasoning with him. He bought his coins, insisted on giving me one of them and by the end of the afternoon the price of gold had dropped. With respect to whatever I may possess at any moment, in cash or kind, prices have gone on dropping ever since.

It was during this period that I encountered a man as weird

in his own way as Ferdinand Lop and a good deal more baffling. An Englishman about fifty years old, I imagine, he was monumentally bulky with a voice that seemed to rumble echoingly around his vast interior before finally emerging. That voice alone was uniquely portentous. The simplest utterance seemed to be charged with significance. Perhaps it was. One always had the impression of something very strange indeed in the background.

His name, precisely because it was so commonplace, likewise gave the curious impression that it was some kind of camouflage. 'John' went awkwardly with his physical rotundity, his sonorous voice, the mysterious comings and goings which I was to observe over the years and the grandiose scale on which he lived. No one could have been less John. Julian, Jocelyn or Jasper, or, better still, Vladimir, Waldemar or Cesare—any of these would have suited him very well but John, no.

Ostensibly he was merely the proprietor of a publishing house which produced books in English for sale exclusively on the Continent, not because of any pornographic content but for copyright reasons. This, however, was manifestly only one of his activities. *Who's Who* listed him, among other things, as one of the directors of the Paris ethnological museum, mention was also made of the fact that he had been military governor of (I think) Jerusalem during the First World War. So what was he—publisher, ethnologist, soldier? Or, as increasingly I was convinced, something very much more enigmatic? I never found out.

There was a lot which I never found out. What was the source of his income, for instance? That was a question to which I and others would have dearly liked to know the answer. His publishing firm, obviously, had been unable to function during the war and had not yet resumed operations. He was nonetheless able to occupy a magnificent private house on the Ile de la Cité. In London, he had equally magnificent chambers in Lincoln's Inn Fields although, as far as I know, he had no connexion with the legal profession. People who had been privileged to see them assured me that his villa in Florence and his apartment in Munich were similarly luxurious. Four such establishments suggested that he was not exactly indigent.

I was once his guest in London for a day or two and observed the furnishings of the Lincoln's Inn chambers with simple wonder—the silver plate from which we ate, the Georgian crystal from which we drank, the Bokhara carpets. These things presumably had to be paid for. So, too, it seemed reasonable to suppose, did the staff which looked after him—the butler, the valet, the cook, the maid, the chauffeur. Then there was the Rolls-Royce which conveyed him on all occasions or possibly the Rolls-Royces, because unless the same car followed him from place to place he must have had one in London and another in Paris and conceivably a third in Florence and a fourth in Munich.

For some reason which I can no longer recall I had occasion to dine with his lawyer at the latter's club. The club port was renowned. At the end of the meal, we verified its reputation, thoroughly. With the fifth or sixth glass, the lawyer forgot the caution which the ethics of his profession should have required him to exercise. Leaning forward as though fearful that his indiscretion might have incalculable consequences and lowering his voice until it was scarcely audible, 'Tell me,' he whispered, 'do you know where John's money comes from?'

'Surely you, as his lawyer, should know better than anyone.'

'Yes, I've been his lawyer for thirty-five years but I haven't the faintest idea.'

'Neither have I.'

Whatever the source of John's money may have been, he fastidiously avoided actually handling the stuff. While I was staying with him in London, I found it necessary to ask if he could lend me five pounds. He looked quite startled. The butler was summoned with a tug on the bell rope. When he appeared, 'Benson' (or whatever his name may have been) 'is there a five-pound note anywhere in the house?'

'Certainly, sir. What would you wish me to do with it?'

'Put it in an envelope, Benson, and give it to Mr Kershaw.'

Thanks to USRAT, I was now in a position to dress in a style that had Nick alternating between unconcealed disgust and derisive laughter. I could not match John's splendour—suit from Savile Row, shirt from Charvet, a luscious tie from Sulka, with a gold watch chain garlanding his prodigious stomach—but I was at least fit to be seen in his company. Whenever his esoteric affairs brought him to Paris he would take me to extravagant meals in one or another of the great restaurants. The prices on the menu were alarming but it was evident that they didn't alarm John. Understandably. He never paid. As we left, the proprietor would approach and inquire anxiously whether everything had been satisfactory. Unless the Romanée-Conti or the *rognons à la liégeoise* had somehow disappointed him, John would let it be known that he was satisfied. Satisfied or not, no bill was in any circumstances presented.

Sam himself would have been envious of John's circle of acquaintances. Greetings with every sort of celebrity or notable were constantly being exchanged in the restaurants where we dined. 'My dear Noël, I hear great reports of your new play' or '*Mais je te vois trop rarement, mon cher Sacha*' or 'Of course I'd be delighted, Duchess' or (because he was seemingly at ease in every European language) '*Guten Abend, Herr Senator, wie geht es Ihnen?*' or '*Caro Federico! Dove stai girando in questo momento?*'

Telegrams were the only means of communication he used. They were remarkable documents and I wish I had preserved them. He disdained to economise in the wording. 'My dear Alister,' they would begin, 'you will, I know, with your customary benignity, excuse my somewhat protracted silence due to circumstances which it is hardly of interest to particularise. Stop. Should you yourself not be excessively occupied next Thursday, perhaps you will give me the pleasure of dining with me at La Perouse. Stop. The good Henri has informed me that he will be able to provide us with a Clos de Tart which, by his always reliable account, is . . .'

One of these Jamesian compositions of his once invited me

to meet him at the Paris airport where he had an hour or two to spend between planes. Full details concerning his flight number and time of arrival were embedded in his sumptuous prose. I inquired at the airline's desk if any delay was anticipated. Worse than a delay, I was told—exceptionally the plane in question was not putting down in Paris but going straight on to Strasbourg or somewhere. This I knew to be impossible. Flights were not altered if John had booked on them, that went without saying. I waited.

Precisely at the hour he had specified a plane put down. Only one passenger emerged. John. He was surrounded by what looked like the entire crew, displaying a markedly uneasy, not to say apprehensive, deference. They accompanied him to where I was waiting and stood there as though awaiting instructions. John dismissed them with a curt nod.

Over our drinks, I mentioned that I had been told his plane would not be putting down. Rumblingly he replied, 'Yes, I myself was given to understand that some such frivolous plan was envisaged.'

'So how . . . ?'

'My dear fellow, these things are very easily arranged.'

'Not by me. What did you do exactly?'

'Why, I merely requested the functionary who informed me of the alteration to despatch a cable for me. "You will send it," I told him, "to Lord Beachampton, chairman of your company. Take this down: My dear Bobby, I am sorry to have to advise you that, owing to the gross incompetence of your staff, I have been put to considerable inconvenience. You will, I know, ensure that the most rigorous disciplinary action is taken against those responsible. Just send that off at once, will you?" Some minutes later it was decided that the plane would be putting down in Paris after all.'

These things are very easily arranged: whether the problem consisted of diverting a plane from its course, obtaining a limitless supply of petrol when it was still rationed or requiring his tailor to come over from London to Paris expressly in order to measure him for a new suit, the phrase was one I heard from him frequently. He used it, I remember, when I had lost a painting of no great value but which for personal reasons was important to me. A friend had looked after it for me during my spell in the streets and was due to return it. She had left it in her car and the car was, inevitably, stolen. The police guffawed at the notion that they might one day recover it. I mentioned the mishap to John.

He asked me one or two questions, then in that subterranean voice which always sounded as though the Almighty were addressing Moses, 'Well, we must see what can be done. These things are very easily arranged as a rule.'

They were arranged this time in some forty-eight hours. I was summoned to the Ile de la Cité by one of the usual convoluted telegrams. On my arrival, 'I fear that your friend's car has lost its number plates,' he announced. 'Car thieves waste no time in attending to that detail. Otherwise, it seems to be unharmed. The painting, I am happy to say, is intact.'

'But, John, this is miraculous. How on earth did you do it?'

'Oh, an inquiry here and an inquiry there. These things are very easily arranged.'

CHAPTER FIVE

The champagne cocktails and the meals at the Grand Véfour didn't last as long as I would have liked. A reorganisation of USRAT took place and it was decided that my contribution to its operations was no longer necessary. It had been unnecessary from the beginning but no one had noticed.

The pleasant American who had hired me in the first place expressed his regrets at having to announce my dismissal. He was clearly surprised, and I think a little put out, by the cheerfulness with which I received the news. Whether, in fact, he was sorry at having to get rid of me I couldn't say; but, amiable as he was, I was delighted to get rid of him. I had a final champagne cocktail to celebrate my liberation. Nick had been absolutely right in her judgment: offices and I were not at ease together.

Freelance translating and journalism, which was what I now took on, didn't bring in enough to maintain me in the sixteenth *arrondissement* but I thought I could do better than Nick's flat or the rue Notre-Dame-des-Champs. Besides, I wanted to get to know a new district. The guidebook cliché about Paris being a conglomeration of villages was an accurate description. Montparnasse, dominated by the Coupole, was one village, Nick's Montmartre was another, the sixteenth *arrondissement* with its counts and be-hatted matrons was a third. But that left seventeen *arrondissements*, seventeen villages, which were virtually unknown territory as far as I was concerned. Someone told me about a room to let on the rue de Charonne in the eleventh. I decided to try that.

You would have had a hard time uncovering any counts in the rue de Charonne. There had been quite a few at one time but their mansions had been demolished long since. During the Terror, counts, not to mention dukes and duchesses, had been even more numerous. The sinister Dr Belhomme had his so-called clinic in the rue de Charonne. There, on payment of what might appropriately be called a princely sum, aristocrats were lodged and provided with certificates attesting that they were too ill to be carted off to the guillotine. But the clinic had also disappeared, as had the various monasteries and convents which were once located in the vicinity.

The rue de Charonne was now a typical nineteenth-century Paris street with no historical or aesthetic lures. For unregenerate lovers of the city like myself, however, it was just because it was so undistinguished, so much a part of the everyday, working Paris that its appeal was irresistible. Narrow alleys ran off it to either side, linking up the murky squares in which were practised those out-of-the-way crafts which had so fascinated me during my first weeks in the city. There were odd little shops which gave the impression that you were the first customer they had had in fifty years. You could buy goods which had long ceased to be produced and which bore forgotten trade names. In one such place I came up on the complex equipment required for the preparation of absinthe. Its production had been prohibited in 1915 but the equipment was still in its original wrappings.

Ill-informed tourists would sometimes make a special trip to the Place de la Bastille which was only a couple of hundred yards away and be disappointed to discover that nothing was left of the old prison. They might traverse the quarter on their way to visit Oscar Wilde's tomb in the Père-Lachaise cemetery which was in the adjoining district. That was all. For the rest, the rue de Charonne and the whole of the eleventh *arrondissement* was French territory.

My room was situated in a forbidding concrete block and was as plebeian as everyone else's. The owner when I asked him about it had assured me that it was furnished and so, technically, it was. It contained a bed, a table and a chair. That was certainly a come-down from the sixteenth *arrondissement* but, compared to Nick's echoing vaults, it could almost be considered excessively cluttered. The walls were as thin as those of the shack in the rue Notre-Dame-des-Champs. From one side I used to hear a young woman emitting reverberating shrieks, yelps, ululations and moanings of ecstasy at unexpected hours both day and night. I used to wonder what prodigious sexual Goliath could have provoked such piercing cries. Returning home one day, I met him as he was leaving his girlfriend's room. He was a rachitic little mannikin with no chin who cringed obsequiously to let me pass. What extraordinary Oriental techniques did he employ to compensate for his puny appearance? 'It's very simple,' said Pierre when I told him of the encounter. 'He's like me, one of the elite—thirty-three centimetres, there's no other explanation. Ask him if you don't believe me.'

On the other side lived a middle-aged couple who had plainly cohabited for longer than either of them would have wished. Perhaps the husband's dimensions were not up to Pierre's standard. It was clear, in any case, that they were not sufficient to engender even a relative harmony in the household, let alone such squeals of delight as my other neighbours produced. All I heard from this disgruntled pair were howls of abuse interspersed with sounds of crockery being smashed, presumably over each other's heads.

Sometimes the brawls and the lovemaking coincided. When the resulting uproar became too much, I would go to the bistro next door. It was exactly the sort of bistro I liked best—smoke-stained ceiling, benches upholstered in worn velvet, a wonderful stench of pastis, tobacco and sweat overlaid with the rich odours of cooking from the minute kitchen at the back, the characteristic Parisian drawl of the customers, the racket of dice thrown exuberantly down on the counter.

Jacques, the owner, was a jovial character although prone to unpredictable and unaccountable outbursts of fury for which he would seek forgiveness by serving drinks all round. We were soon on excellent terms. As in the past, I could borrow money, run up a bill, receive messages (needless to say, I had no telephone) and cadge cigarettes. There was a bonus, too. One of my journalistic activities consisted of providing snippets for the Australian Broadcasting Commission, as it then was. In dealing with recent fashions or some similarly frivolous topic I had no trouble. I could always lift the information I needed from the newspapers. It was when my employers demanded an informed commentary on more serious matters that I felt unsure of myself. Especially in the field of politics I was expected to make forecasts and for someone who didn't know what had happened last week still less what was going to happen next week, this posed problems.

None of my forecasts so far had been too catastrophically wrong but it was obvious that my luck could not continue indefinitely. It was Jacques who saved me from disaster. On my way to the studio one morning I dropped in on him for a cup of coffee.

'What misinformation are you giving your listeners today?'

'I'm forecasting the results of the referendum.'

'That ought to be good for a laugh. And just what is your forecast?'

'Seventy-five per cent in favour.'

'Are you crazy? Fifty-five per cent at the outside.'

After all, I said to myself, Jacques's guess is likely to be better than mine—anybody's is. I scratched out seventy-five on my script and replaced it with fifty-five. When, a week later, the results were announced, Jacques's prediction—ostensibly, mine—proved bang right. Thereafter, all my forecasts came straight from Jacques. They were amazingly accurate on the whole. I acquired quite a reputation.

Having decided, after much timorous hesitation, that neither bloody revolution nor an invasion by the Soviet army was imminent, foreigners were once again to be seen everywhere. Or almost everywhere. Not in my part of Paris. I had the distinction when I first arrived of being the only foreign resident of the rue de Charonne if not of the whole *arrondissement*.

Later on, an American artist was inexplicably impelled to settle in what I had come to regard as my personal fief. At first, I resented his intrusion but when I met him by chance in Jacques's café he turned out to be agreeable company. He was also indescribably credulous which made him a source of continuous pleasure. It was impossible to resist seeing just what absurdities he could be induced to believe.

Taking a cigarette between his lips one day, he said 'Lend me your lighter, will you?'

I contorted my face into an expression of complete incomprehension. 'My *what*, George? My lighter, did you say?'

'Yes, your cigarette lighter.'

'Oh, I see—you mean a mechanical match, I take it.'

'Jesus, I've never heard it called that before.'

'Possibly not, George. But not all of us have adopted the more vulgar Americanisms. Do try to remember—it's a mechanical match.'

For months afterwards, until some compassionate soul put him right, George would periodically come out with, 'Let me have your lighter—God, sorry! I mean your mechanical match.'

I made a number of other sympathetic acquaintances at Jacques's café. Like most Frenchmen of no matter what background the customers were impressed by my claim to be a writer. It was a claim I could now make with rather more justification than in the past. My job with the Americans (as they eventually realised) had left me plenty of spare time and I had actually completed and published a book. I was called on to display it for the admiration of the café's regular clients. For some reason, Armand, a gigantic truck driver, was more dazzled than the others. He was openly eager to have a copy. I gave him one inscribed *'Pour mon pote Armand'* and thereafter he carried it with him on all occasions, proudly directing the attention of anyone he could buttonhole to my inscription. He didn't, naturally, know any English but in spite of this—*'because* of this, you mean,' Alain commented offensively—he was tireless in expounding its merits. 'One of the great books of our time,' he would proclaim with authority, 'an authentic masterpiece.'

Léon was another valued friend. We met in inauspicious circumstances. I was with a couple of fellow Australians one evening. Overhearing us talking in English, Léon, at the bar and having drunk even more than usual, proceeded to deliver himself of a disobliging monologue.

'*Salauds d'étrangers*—bloody foreigners. Nobody asked them to come here . . . pinch our girls . . . get in the way . . . make a bloody nuisance of themselves . . . talking their bloody silly languages . . . go back home . . . '

His grumbling maledictions became monotonous. I went over to the bar. 'Listen, I don't give a damn what you think of foreigners but you're beginning to get on my nerves. So shut up.'

However drunk he might be, Léon was never belligerent except verbally. 'But you misunderstand, Monsieur,' he said in tones of dignified astonishment, 'I had no intention of annoying you. True, I don't like foreigners but you, I know, are a Canadian and Canadians are different. They talk French like us.'

From then on, I was a Canadian. It was impossible to convince Léon otherwise. '*Vive les Canadiens*,' he would cry whenever I entered the café, '*Vive Québec!*'

There is a story in *Three Men in a Boat* about a man springing out of bed in the middle of a winter night under the impression that it was morning and time to go to work. Léon once figured in an identical incident. He and Jacques and I had drunk a satisfactory amount of wine together one Sunday afternoon. What Léon had had to drink earlier I couldn't say. Presumably a lot since about five o'clock, when it was already beginning to get dark, he announced that he was going home to have a snooze. I stayed on with Jacques.

A couple of hours later we saw Léon hurtling past. He had exchanged his Sunday finery for workday overalls and was making for the métro station. Jacques and I looked at each other in bewilderment. After a while Léon reappeared. 'Give me a drink,' he ordered, and while he was waiting uttered a protracted string of curses.

'Why the overalls, Léon?' we asked.

Exactly like Jerome's character, it appeared, Léon had gone

to sleep, woken up, glanced at the clock and had seen that it was seven o'clock. Immediately assuming in his still befuddled state that it was seven o'clock in the morning, he had leapt out of bed, had cut himself shaving, had nearly broken a leg as he raced downstairs and had arrived at the métro in a foul temper, out of breath and with a stitch in his side. He had presented his weekly ticket.

'This isn't valid until tomorrow,' the man at the gate told him.

'What the hell do you mean? It's valid from Monday, isn't it?'

'That's right.'

'Well, it's Monday, isn't it?'

'No, it's Sunday—7.30 on Sunday evening.'

Of all my friends in the rue de Charonne, Madame Gustin headed the list. She was considerably older than I so that I always addressed her respectfully as Madame Gustin while she called me Alister. It became the custom for me to drop in at her ironmonger's shop most evenings when she would send her delivery boy next door to get us a couple of glasses of pastis. We would drink these at her counter while she recounted the happenings of the day with immense verve and humour.

Some of these happenings I witnessed myself. I came in one evening to find her on her knees scrutinising the floor where her dog had just made a mess. 'What on earth are you looking for, Madame Gustin?'

'A thousand-franc note.'

'But are you likely to find a thousand-franc note in a pile of dog shit?'

'Well, this afternoon I dropped the note on the floor and this larcenous animal grabbed hold of it and swallowed it. Even if I don't get the note back, I'm hoping he'll have enough decency to give me back some change.'

I only once saw her other than cheerful. Her second husband had recently died and been buried in the same tomb as her first. Now, her second husband's family wanted the body transferred to the provincial town where he had been born. Madame

Gustin had been present at the disinterment and the grisly operation had understandably left her feeling low-spirited.

In answer to my solicitous inquiry, she told me how she had passed the afternoon but omitted to explain the reason for the exhumation.

'How very painful for you, Madame Gustin. But why was the disinterment necessary?'

'Because,' she said, her genuine distress evaporating at the prospect of making a good joke, 'because my second husband kept quarrelling with my first and the neighbours complained about the noise.'

She herself once came close to hearing complaints from the neighbours. Reasonably soon after her husband's death she acquired a boyfriend—an especially incongruous term since he was a man of about her own age, which was in the early sixties. He was thoroughly boyish, however, when it came to enjoying himself. I dined with them several times in Madame Gustin's flat and have rarely experienced such uninhibited boisterousness.

I was not with them one evening when they celebrated her birthday with an inordinate quantity of champagne. At about two o'clock in the morning, the boyfriend had reached the singing stage. I had heard him singing before. His notion of melody was uncertain but he could produce an astonishing volume of sound. By Madame Gustin's account, he outdid himself in honour of her birthday. She was surprised, she said, that I hadn't heard him, that the whole quarter hadn't heard him.

Next morning she left her flat with the knowledge that all her acting talents were going to be required. Sure enough, on the stairs she came face to face with the woman who lived a couple of floors below. She looked as if she'd been waiting for this opportunity. Before she could speak, Madame Gustin seized the initiative and plunged into a bravura performance.

Majestic, oozing outraged gentility, her voice trembling with indignation, 'Good morning, Madam Dupont,' she said. 'I'm sure you must have heard that disgusting racket last night. I didn't get a wink of sleep. Monstrous! If I could only find out who was the ruffian responsible . . . '

'Why, Madame Gustin, I must admit I thought the noise was coming from your flat.'

'From *my* flat! Good heavens, do you think I would tolerate such behaviour in *my* flat? *I* have to work—*I* must get my rest, not listen to drunkards bellowing all night.'

Nobody could match Madame Gustin in protraying affronted dignity. It was one of her favourite roles. The neighbour was instantly convinced of her innocence. The two of them shook their heads over the scandal, agreeing that every effort must be made to identify the culprit and obtain reparation.

Her ebullience notwithstanding, Madame Gustin was an excellent businesswoman. While we were drinking our aperitifs one evening, a customer came in and asked for product X.

'As you wish, Monsieur,' said Madame Gustin, 'as you wish. You're entitled to buy whatever product you choose.' Her expression was that of somebody who felt she had no choice but to let people make their own blunders and perhaps learn from them.

'It doesn't sound as if you thought very highly of product X,' the customer observed.

'I? But, my dear sir, it doesn't matter what I think. You ask for product X and that's all there is to it.'

'Come, come, what's the matter with it?'

'Oh, far be it from me to criticise any brand. All I can say is that I personally would never dream of using anything but product Y.'

'Well, you're in the business and should know. I'll take a packet of product Y.'

'I can assure you, my dear sir, you won't regret it' and, as the door closed behind the customer, 'Of course, there isn't an atom of difference between them, Alister. Only I didn't happen to have any product X in stock.'

An excellent businesswoman but friends always had priority over money-making. She proved it, overwhelmingly, when she enabled me to escape from the combined hullaballoo of copulation and domestic warfare which regularly drove me out of my room.

'You can't go on living in that wretched hovel, Alister, it's perfectly ridiculous. I was discussing the matter with Jacques and we agreed that it is no place for a writer, an artist. You must move to something very much better.'

Given the housing shortage and my financial state, one could only treat that sort of proposal as fantasy and make a jocular rejoinder.

'Fine, Madame Gustin. If you can find me a flat in this quarter, because I don't want to live anywhere else, with, say, four rooms, at the pegged rent, no key money to be paid, and a three-year lease with option of renewal—why, I'll move tomorrow.' As things then were (and still are) I might equally reasonably have stood out for the Elysée palace.

Madame Gustin's intelligence network covered the entire district. Even so, there was something almost uncanny about the feat she now brought off. I was summoned by her delivery boy to present myself at the shop. Almost anyone in Paris would have been prepared to pay a good many thousands of francs for the information which was now given to me for nothing. 'You'd better start packing.'

'You don't mean you've found a place?'

'Certainly. It has six rooms not four but otherwise it meets all your specifications.'

'Nearby?'

'A hundred yards from your present slum.'

It might have been John himself casually recovering a stolen motor car.

The only problem with my new flat was that the furniture situation was identical with that in Nick's apartment. Every single item had, quite legitimately, been removed by the previous occupants apart from a thick layer of dirt throughout the place.

I had had plenty of cause over the years to appreciate just how far removed were the French from the spiteful image of them propagated by the dedicated francophobes. Nonetheless, I was unprepared for what now happened. Jacques's waitress, dumpy, energetic, smiling Andrée, had her Wednesdays off. The Wednesday after the new flat became mine, I was contemplating the disaster area when Andrée came bustling in.

'*Mon Dieu*! What sort of pigs lived here? Never mind, Monsieur Alister, I'll have it cleaned up for you in no time.'

'But, Andrée, I can't afford to pay you.'

'Who said anything about payment?'

She turned up regularly thereafter whenever she had a spare hour or two. Perhaps not in no time but with remarkable rapidity she had scrubbed the place to within an inch of its life. 'Now I'll make you some curtains,' she told me, 'I've got some material at home that's just lying there.'

Jacques was another contributor to my comfort. He brought a café table and two chairs with him. Léon's present was an ancient mattress and a kettle. 'I wouldn't do it for an ordinary foreigner but you're a Canadian and Canadians are different.' There was a kitchen tap which dripped maddeningly and incurably. Armand attended to that. I've forgotten—unforgiveably—all the others who one way or another helped to install me. Half the inhabitants of the rue de Charonne must have contributed. And if the whole story sounds like a sentimental fairytale (which I'm sure it does) I can't do anything about it. That's what happened.

The move didn't detach me from the rue de Charonne. Madame Gustin had borne in mind my stipulation and the new flat was just around the corner on the Boulevard Voltaire. So I continued to drink an aperitif each evening in her shop, to tell Léon about life in Québec, to play dice with Armand and to get invaluable political tips for my broadcasts from Jacques.

Only one thing had changed. My room in the rue de Charonne had been about eight feet square. I couldn't invite anyone there. One extra person and it felt as crowded as a métro station at rush hour. In any case, if the erotomaniacs on one side and the warring couple on the other were simultaneously in action, conversation would have been made impossible by their combined shrieks of delight and savage recriminations.

Now I could have as many visitors as I liked. When I hung the chimney-hook (since French houses are decently heated you don't have a housewarming) I invited about thirty (glasses by courtesy of Jacques, service by Andrée). They were a sort of *bouillabaisse* of personalities presided over by Madame Gustin at her most queenly: Léon and Armand and other residents of the rue de Charonne, the Count from my sixteenth *arrondissement* days, the unpredictable Alain, Monsieur Robert from the Coupole, the local doctor, Nick, the enigmatic John (midway between one unrevealed rendezvous and another), with a few actors and writers I'd met at the Coupole. My party was a great success. Alain managed to slip a paragraph into his paper identifying Léon and Armand and the other rue de Charonne guests by name and attributing to each of them enormous artistic, scientific or social standing. Léon, I recall, was described as a leading Canadian sociologist. He was stunned and, on recovering, rapturous at seeing his name in print. Only what, he asked me, was a sociologist? I told him, truthfully, that I didn't know.

The hanging of the chimney-hook had a particular significance for me. I hadn't realised it at the time but living for so long in furnished rooms, in Louis's hotel, in the Montparnasse rabbit hutch, in Nick's sacked apartment, in my sixteenth *arrondissement* grandeur and under the bridges of the Seine had made me obscurely uneasy. That vagrant existence had given me the feeling that I had only a tenuous hold on Paris, that I might at any moment against my will be whisked away. Now for the first time I was a legal tenant not a sub-tenant, I had a formal not an uncertain verbal lease, my own name not the proprietor's figured in the telephone directory. None of it should have mattered but it did. At last I could relax. I belonged.

CHAPTER SIX

The eleventh *arrondissement* may have been a comedown from the sixteenth but my new flat was superior to anything I'd had before. Except for Nick's vast residence I'd never lived in anything so spacious in all the years I'd been in Paris—quite a number of them by this time. Enough to make me, in my own eyes if in no one else's, as much a Parisian as Armand or Léon or Jacques. I looked superciliously on other foreigners established for only two or three years in the city, hobnobbing exclusively with their fellow countrymen, still persuaded that they'd get typhoid if they drank tap water, confident that every waiter or shopkeeper was trying to cheat them and incapable of getting from the Boulevard St Germain to the Champs-Elysées without a protracted examination of maps.

Most of them, anyway, were in Paris for fixed periods, on assignment as executives for foreign firms or as embassy personnel or functionaries in some international organisation. Sooner or later they would be leaving. I was never going to leave. So time didn't mean the same thing to them as to me. They measured the number of weeks or months left to them whereas I wasn't even aware that years were going by until one day a newly met acquaintance asked me how long I'd been in France. Naturally, she wasn't in the least interested. Why should she have been? Her question was simply a routine banality. If I'd answered without thinking, I imagine I would have said, 'Oh, five or six years—something like that.' But I made a quick calculation and if the result elicited no more from my acquaintance than a languid, 'Oh, really?', it left me stupefied, incredulous. Not five or six—My God! Twenty!

This discovery more or less coincided with the gloomy realisation that my great love affair was over. For me it had been supremely glamorous, a genuine once-in-a-lifetime affair.

Now the doubts and anxieties, the longings, the quarrels and reconciliations, the roses and raptures were finished. Paris and I had ceased to be lovers. We were a married couple. We felt the irritable affection for each other that comes about from mere propinquity over a long period but there was nothing else left. Divorce, I could see, was unavoidable.

The usual well-meaning idiots tried to bring us together again. Passionate love, they explained gently and reasonably, was something which only the young could experience. It might be hard to accept but I was no longer very young. I didn't find it in the least hard to accept. My lines and wrinkles didn't worry me. It was the fact that Paris had none which I found insupportable. She was older than I, she already had her share of lines and wrinkles when we first met. I had begun by not noticing them. Later on I saw them and loved them. Now she had undergone, was still undergoing, a horrifying facelift. Externally, at any rate, she bore no resemblance to the city which had so effortlessly seduced me.

Fiacres didn't go clip-clopping along the boulevards any more. They wouldn't have clip-clopped for long in any case. Cars had taken possession and Parisians didn't drive cars so much as brandish them. They were a weapon of mass extermination. When I first arrived in Paris you could cross the Place de la Concorde or the Place de l'Etoile with your eyes closed and be sure of reaching the other side without a scratch. For years now I myself wouldn't have tried to cross either Place except with an armed escort.

In the eyes of their owners, moreover, the cars were simultaneously weapons and cuddlesome little things to be cherished and protected. Put the smallest dint in a Parisian's car and he or she would promptly go berserk. What you got was not jocular abuse in the manner of Pierre. You were subjected to threats of petrifying virulence and you could take it that God was on your side if these were not immediately followed by physical reprisals.

That wasn't the worst of it. The detestable vehicles were looked on not just as weapons and pets but as tribal jujus to be propitiated at all costs. Or, more exactly, as sacred cows permitted to roam unchecked wherever they might choose, to block streets, to take over footpaths from the surviving pedestrians. One outstandingly barmy visionary proposed in all seriousness that the Seine should be roofed over so that a giant motor highway might be constructed above it. I never understood why the authorities rejected the plan. Schemes no less crack-brained were adopted with enthusiasm.

Street singers had become as wholly extinct as the fiacres. Nobody would have had the patience to stand around and listen. They used to accompany themselves on the accordion. That was the quintessential sound of Paris. You heard it on street corners, in the corridors of the métro, in shabby dance halls. The tunes were sometimes bouncy, sometimes melancholy. Bouncy or melancholy, you couldn't love Paris and not love 'the poor man's piano'. But it had become as anachronistic as the serpent or the sackbut. What you heard in its place was the guitar, clawed at by dishevelled larrikins from Bermondsey or the Bronx who harassed captive audiences on café terraces. The passing traffic at least had the merit of rendering their haphazard plunking somewhat less audible.

The very odours of the city had changed. Naturally, it was the stink of exhaust fumes which predominated but what had us sentimentalists whimpering was that the small perfumes which used to be so endearingly a part of Paris had gone. Coffee was one of them. It seemed to me that the aroma of the coffee served in the cafés was no longer the same. No café proprietor would have had the nerve to dish up instant coffee but that was what it smelt like. By the same token, you were more likely to catch a whiff of American or English cigarettes than the full-bodied smell of Gitanes or Gauloises. Instead of sniffing the bountiful odours of *choucroute* or *gras double à la lyonnaise* as you walked along the street, the chances were that you'd recoil from the reek of hamburgers. Fast-food 'outlets' were everywhere.

So were drug stores. They were of a flamboyance which made their American progenitors look pitifully dowdy. Ornate

metal curlicues, multicoloured overhead lamps, benches upholstered in imitation leather and plenty of plastic were standard
features of the interior decoration. The specialities, apart from
crypto-omelettes and synthetic sandwiches, were mountainous
ice-creams topped with little American flags.

I couldn't decide which revolted me more, the fake American
drug stores or the spurious English pubs which began to
pullulate about the same time. Neither had anything in
common with decent cafés. But they were triumphing. More
and more, the decent cafés were closing down. When you
reached some cherished establishment and saw that it was still
there you felt a mixture of relief and incredulity.

The inevitable idiots came up with their inevitable explanation. My surly objection to the changes which had taken
place was additional proof that I was getting old. The old,
as was well known, couldn't endure changes. I thought myself
that I could cope with changes—certain changes—quite
adequately. And while there was no denying that I was getting
older, the real problem was that Paris was getting younger or,
rather, was getting newer—intolerably, revoltingly newer. The
facelifting proceeded inexorably.

Pierre, an intransigently chauvinistic Parisian, abhorred the
cosmetic surgery from which his city was suffering as much
as I did. His invective whenever some new abomination
revealed itself was usually of a dazzling obscenity although
every so often he employed a denunciatory style of almost
biblical grandeur. The vituperation which he had taught me
to direct at pedestrians and incompetent drivers was friendly
banter compared to the maledictions he pronounced as we
toured Paris on foot or in his taxi. He preferred the taxi; it
enabled us to make a quicker getaway from the monstrosities.
'Taxpayer's money,' he would mutter as we confronted the
latest blood-curdling monument, '*my* money. I don't mind
seeing shit but I can't stand seeing shit that I've had to pay
for. Next thing you know they'll be introducing a special shit
tax, the *salauds*.'

Over the drinks with which we tried to expunge the memory

of the shit, we would speculate as to the origin of the process which was ostensibly rejuvenating Paris and in fact putting it to death. Two or three years earlier the Student Revolution— or as Pierre invariably termed it, the Tiny Tots' Revolution— had had the country's rulers displaying a pusillanimity which surprised even those of us who had never held them in high regard. Pierre had a theory that it was the Tiny Tots' Revolution which had caused the cosmeticians to get to work on the face of Paris. He may well have been right. While the 'Revolution' was taking place, we had sometimes gone along to the Latin Quarter to watch the pubescent demonstrators carrying on. As militant anarchists, they were unimpressive. Their uniform consisted of bemired jeans, bicycle chains and unravelled pullovers but it was nonetheless a uniform. And there was something depressing about the way in which they chanted their vacuous slogans with military precision. It would have been a relief if only someone had come in one syllable behind the others. No such luck. They might have been the Young Pioneers baying in unison at a May Day parade. And what they were baying embodied yet another constant. Every one of their slogans, as Pierre pointed out, unfailingly contained the word 'new'. When they were not shouting shrilly for a new educational system, they were asserting their right to a new society, a new morality, a new outlook, even, poor loons, a new world.

All of them ended up in one of the good old profitable professions as bankers, notaries and industrialists. Meantime, they were engaged in turning a simple monosyllable into an incantation. From then on, any product—a magazine, a political party, a religion or a vacuum cleaner—could be successfully marketed so long as it described itself as new. *La nouvelle cuisine* furnished a perfect example. How enthusiastically the simpletons gobbled it up! They were just as hungry at the end of the meal as when they sat down but their consolation was the knowledge that it was not a commonplace hunger, not the hunger with which the *clochards* were familiar. This was a *new* hunger and the simpletons relished every pang.

'I'll tell you what's new about the new cuisine,' Pierre remarked, tucking into a robust *hachis parmentier* at one of our unrepentantly old bistros, 'you get ten times less food for ten times more money.'

None of this much mattered. After all, one was not compelled—for the moment, at any rate—to content oneself with half-a-dozen disconsolate peas huddled beside a bite-size morsel of meat. One was not compelled to join the new party, read the new magazine or remove dust with the new vacuum cleaner. But the novelty-freaks were resolved that Paris itself should be renewed, renovated, neatly trimmed, smartened up. The nation's governing geriatrics, eager to show that they were new at heart, ordered structures of steadily increasing squalor and absurdity to be erected. There were even ministers of newness (euphemistically designated ministers of culture) whose willingness, not to say eagerness, to be bamboozled by every kind of architectural or artistic confidence man was unlimited.

Paris and I were divorced by the time the culminating aberration—except that there was every reason to suppose that worse was to come—came into existence. We had parted on fairly amiable terms, though, and occasionally saw each other. During one of our meetings I glimpsed the aberration. It was a gigantic glass pyramid. Nobody ever explained why the neophiles should imagine that this supremely primitive form was excitingly 'new' but up it went. The site chosen was bang in front of the Louvre: the neophiles always enjoyed plumping down their bric-à-brac where it would disfigure something 'old'.

Then there was the Beaubourg Cultural Centre. That was a real treat. Nothing about the Centre bore any resemblance to a building conceived by rational beings and the responsible zanies were apparently captivated by the notion of having the thing's guts, so to speak, prominently displayed. In particular, its façade was horrendously decorated with garishly painted pipes and tubes although we never discovered whether these were for purposes of ventilation or sewage disposal or had no other purpose than to symbolise newness. Pierre looked at the mad array with gloomy appraisal. He always had a carrying voice. He now raised it further to make sure that the surrounding worshippers would hear his judgment. 'You know what it looks like? It looks like the aftermath of a hysterectomy.'

Les Halles, the great central market, was a natural target for the Pariscides. It was everything they most loathed—chaotic, animated, tumbledown, vivid, meandering. It was also insalubrious. That gave the new brooms their excuse—not that they ordinarily bothered to offer one. They could not, they explained, tolerate anything so noxious a moment longer. Well, nobody could dispute that the market was messy. Hillocks of discarded meat, decayed fruit and vegetable scraps grew waist-high as the night wore on and innumerable rats wouldn't have lived anywhere else. I agreed with the rats. A little squalor never hurt anyone. Plague had never broken out there, nobody had died from the defective hygienic arrangements. Part of the charm of Les Halles lay, precisely, in its mediaeval dirt and turmoil. All of us loved the flaring lights, the yelling of the porters lugging sides of beef or mountainous crates of fruit on their shoulders, the glittering all-night cafés and restaurants, the good-humoured whores, the bargaining between buyers and sellers which added appreciably to the prevailing din, the shuttling of barrows, the occasional brawls.

My periodic spells as an odd-job man in Les Halles had given me an extra attachment to the place. Moreover, I enjoyed a high distinction in market circles. I had been made an honorary member of the confraternity of wholesale butchers. My sponsor was Le Petit Louis, six feet tall and of massive build.

Le Petit Louis was a figure of consequence in Les Halles. And even outside. I took him back with me once for dinner, stopping on the way to buy some steaks. The butcher laid them before me for my approval. They looked first-rate to me. Not, however, to Le Petit Louis. Eyeing them sorrowfully, he addressed the butcher without annoyance, almost with commiseration. 'No, no, my poor friend. You haven't quite understood. We want steaks to *eat*.'

The butcher expostulated with vehemence. His meat was known throughout the district for its impeccable quality. Never before had any client suggested otherwise. If we were not satisfied . . . Le Petit Louis raised an imperious hand. 'Do you know, my friend, on whom you are attempting to unload this offal? *Je suis Le Petit Louis.*' The butcher blenched. Without replying he retired behind the scenes. When he returned it was with steaks which even I could see were of a different order.

A miniature copper saucepan attested to my acceptance by the wholesaler butchers' guild. It had to be carried at all times. If you were called on to produce it by a fellow member and were unable to comply, you were required to buy drinks for everyone present. As an honorary butcher, a protégé of Le Petit Louis, and with my saucepan in my pocket, the news that the market was to be demolished hit me harder than the construction of the cultural centre, pipes and all.

Demolished it was, though, and for some years was replaced by a vast waterlogged canyon while the minister of newness pondered over the problem of what to put there. In the end, a bleak congeries of prim boutiques and hamburger stalls was decided on. Even the rats kept well away from it. Once again, I was on the side of the rats.

Some landmarks were permitted to survive, of course. The Coupole, for one, had remained its old self. But it was an island. Next door, the Dôme had been 'done over' by an interior decorator with nothing to lose. Customers were lodged in discreet cubicles. Every table had its shaded lamp. The ambience was a deeply unattractive blend of gentility and raffishness. Ferdinand Lop, Monsieur de Beauharnais and Monsieur Dupont would have suffocated there. So would I.

Across the road, the Rotonde had been similarly debased. For a start, it had been carved in two. One half had become a cinema. A list of names reminiscent of a war memorial was engraved on the cinema's walls. These were the artists and writers, from Arp to Zadkine, who had frequented the Rotonde before its brutal bisection.

Further down the boulevard, 'developers' (what they developed in me was an unconquerable queasiness), with the benediction of the politicians, had razed the old Gare de Montparnasse. It had been a charming artefact, like a railway station in the provinces. There was a little bar at street level where a white wine of exceptional merit was available. That was also where to go if you were looking for the best cider in Paris because it was at the Gare de Montparnasse that passengers arrived from Brittany. You could always be sure of hearing plenty of juicy Breton accents in the vicinity. They were still to be heard but, under the new dispensation, the Bretons disembarked at a painfully different station, a sullen construction conceived with such attention to efficiency as to make it all but impossible to find one's way around in it. I never heard that exceptional white wine or cider could be had there.

The ultimate warning that the moment had arrived to run for cover came from Ménilmontant, only a few kilometres from the rue de Charonne. Ménilmontant was the very heart of unfashionable Paris. Anyone born there had a fair claim to be considered more Parisian than other Parisians. My truck driver friend Armand had established his pre-eminence in the rue de Charonne merely by insisting on the fact that he and his forebears for three generations had been born in Ménilmontant. Reminding opponents of his lineage enabled him to come out on top in any argument. '*Toi*,' he would sneer at some poor brute whose family had their roots in Montmartre or Auteuil or, worse still, the suburbs, 'what do you know about it anyway? *Nous autres de Ménilmontant . . .* '

Poor old Armand! It was heartbreaking to see the change in him when he heard that the bureaucrats had plans for his native quarter. Usually, no one could have been more jovial than Armand. I wouldn't have thought anything could get him down. But the prospect of seeing the steep cobbled streets of Ménilmontant lined with smart boutiques and expensive restaurants was too much for him. In the past when we met he had always greeted me with genial smiles and claps on the shoulder and commands to join him in a glass of wine. Not any more. He drank alone and with solemnity. And he no longer made the pilgrimage to Ménilmontant as he had done every Sunday ever since I knew him.

With these horrors all around us, there was no reason to hope that the rue de Charonne would be spared. When I was more than ordinarily depressed about what was going on I used to wonder for how long it would even continue to bear its name. Already the Allée du Roule had been baptised the Avenue Franklin-D-Roosevelt, the Place de l'Etoile had been the Place de L'Etoile since the early eighteenth century. His admirers had renamed it the Place du Général De Gaulle. A hundred metres from the rue de Charonne was the Place Voltaire. Voltaire was someone for whom I had a particular veneration. It shocked me when his Place became the Place Léon Blum.

For the moment the rue de Charonne was allowed to retain its name but that was the only satisfaction offering. New and detestable buildings were thrown up, half the little squares and alleys were torn apart in conformity with the planners' constant preoccupation with hygiene. Even before the process was completed, the old inhabitants began to move out. Madame Gustin was the first to go. Over seventy by this time, she had a third marriage in active preparation and her future husband lived in the country. 'I don't suppose the two of us will do much frolicking naked in the woods,' she told me with an engaging leer, 'but I'll be glad to get away. I never thought I'd want to leave Paris. Seventy years, *tu te rends compte*? Only the rue de Charonne isn't the same any more.'

Indeed it wasn't. Like my neighbours, I had in the past recognised and exchanged salutations with practically everyone I passed in the street. Now half the faces were unfamiliar. Logically the newcomers should have been refugees from Ménilmontant drawn to the eleventh *arrondissement* as the next best thing. We would have felt abashed in their presence but at the same time flattered at their condescension. Apparently, however, they had chosen to stick on in their own quarter, disfigured as it might be. The invaders came from all over the place, not always from Paris, not always from anywhere in France.

Once upon a time I had been the only foreigner for miles around. I rather enjoyed my unique status. Now Portuguese and Arabic and unknown African tongues were as commonly heard in the rue de Charonne as French. Progressively the new arrivals transformed our street into a fief of their own. They disregarded our semi-rural style, our habit of saying a cordial '*Bonjour*' to anyone we met whether we knew him or not. The newcomers looked uneasy if we saluted them.

It was not just in the rue de Charonne that the population had undergone a bewildering transformation. That Portuguese and Africans should be unlike the previous inhabitants was understandable. What was more upsetting was that Parisians themselves were becoming unrecognisable. I had first known them in the period immediately after the war. Life wasn't easy. Rationing, for one thing, was still in force. There were tickets for everything from cauliflowers to caviar. Not that they were of much use. None of the various goodies was available outside the black market. We used to throw most of our tickets away.

The only ones I can recall keeping were bread tickets. These had to be handed over in order to get a loaf from the baker or to order a sandwich in a café. The bread was made from corn. It was bright yellow in colour and it tasted revolting. Coffee was made from powdered acorns or dried cabbage stalks or something—I can't remember what. That, too, tasted horribly. If you were a friend of the house, the *patron* might slip you a saccharine tablet with which to sweeten it. Trains ran spasmodically, letters took a week for delivery a hundred metres away. Housing was a problem. So was clothing. So was everything else.

Despite all the irksome restrictions and irritations, Parisians still deserved their reputation for courtesy. The customer at the Dôme who had managed to keep a straight face when I made my first comical attempts to speak French was typical of the French then. Bureaucrats received you civilly when you presented yourself at their windows. Shop assistants were never too busy to serve you.

People were relaxed. They walked in a leisurely way along

the boulevards. They got their work done without unnecessary fuss and when it was over had time to drink an aperitif with their friends. If you asked someone in the street for directions he would actually stop and do his best to answer you. Laughter still existed.

In the years since then those earnest young executives at whom we used to jeer when they entered the Coupole seemed to have proliferated. You saw them everywhere, armed with briefcases and wearing agonised expressions as they conferred together in secretive little groups. They spoke English with an American accent, sometimes even among themselves. Those Parisians who weren't executives gave the impression of trying to behave like executives, at any rate to the extent of never smiling and being perpetually in a hurry. The loud undignified laughter in which my friends and I used to indulge was rarely heard any more.

The functionaries who had once been quite amiable had realised that they were the top dogs, representatives of the omnipotent State. They had ceased to be in any degree amiable. They disliked being importuned by the rabble and made their feelings clear. To find Parisians of the old polite, helpful and cheerful variety you had to go somewhere like the rue de Charonne. And now there was an exodus even from the rue de Charonne . . .

Jacques sold his café. His successor was a dour-looking individual. One of Jacques's endearing customs consisted of waiting until casual customers had taken their leave and then lowering the shutters so that those of us who remained could roister uninterrupted. I couldn't see the lugubrious new owner facilitating our sprees. He had the air of a man who would turn the lights off and start piling up chairs when he thought we'd stayed long enough. I seriously doubted, too, whether he'd be inclined to lend me money at the end of the month. As for supplying political prophecies for my broadcasts, he was clearly incapable of doing so and I would not have felt encouraged to ask him.

I don't know whether it was the renovation of the quarter

which drove Léon out. Probably not. Nonetheless, he left. We had a final drink together. 'All these foreigners,' said Léon, 'I couldn't stand it another minute. *Bande de vaches*! Of course, you're a Canadian—that's another matter. Canadians are like us, they speak French. *Vive les Canadiens! Vive les Québécois!*' That was that. We would keep in touch, of course, and of course we never did. The old fraternity of the rue de Charonne was at an end.

CHAPTER SEVEN

I knew perfectly well that my lamentations about the deface-
ment of Paris were exaggerated. Part of the huffing and puffing
was for the fun of the thing. Pierre and Alain and I, with one
or two others, got a lot of pleasure out of competing to see
who could curse the neophiles with the most vigour and
originality. We liked meeting in the Coupole and—at the top
of our voices—making plans to blow up the ministry of
newness and the Cultural Centre along with it. The more staid
customers looked disapproving but among the habitués we had
a majority of enthusiastic supporters. Monsieur de Beauharnais
was our chief ally, as was only natural, but Ferdinand Lop was
also on our side. When he extended the Boulevard St Michel
to the coast, he assured us, every precaution would be taken
to ensure that nothing of historical or architectural value was
in any way endangered.

We were glad to hear it because quite a number of sites and
buildings of historical or architectural value were indeed still
intact and it was nice to think that if Lop had his way they'd
go on being intact. Not everything had been disfigured or
destroyed. The officially authorised wreckers had not had time
to carry out their mission in its entirety. You might have to
avoid looking to the right (where there was probably an
international congress centre) or the left (where in all likelihood
a helicoidal repository for municipal archives had been erected)
but if you looked straight ahead you could see something of
Paris as it used to be. Although not always, even then. Looking
straight ahead up the Champs-Elysées, for example, you saw
the Arc de Triomphe transformed into a frame for the cloud-
capp'd subskyscrapers of La Défense, a grisly complex which
the neophiles considered one of their proudest achievements.
Adding it all up—La Défense, the newyorkified Gare de

Montparnasse, the lunatic Cultural Centre, the pubs and drugstores and, more than anything else, the desecration of the rue de Charonne—I decided that I'd had enough. Like Madame Gustin, I'd never anticipated leaving Paris but the time had clearly come.

It wasn't only for my own sake that I was ready to make a bolt for safety. I had remarried and had two children. They had to be rescued, too. There was no knowing what dire psychological consequences might result if they were forced to spend their formative years among the architectural trash. Worse still was the possibility that they might learn to love the neophiles' confections. What if they were to be caught writing covert fan letters to the minister of newness?

A refuge was waiting. Years before, during my affluent period with USRAT, I had bought a small house in the country. So far, I had only occupied it at irregular intervals, intervals that had grown lengthier and lengthier as Paris grew more and more like a gimcrack Brasilia. Henceforward, it would be occupied permanently.

It wasn't by any means the sort of house I would have chosen for myself. City-dwellers—and I'd been one all my life—expect country cottages to be picturesque. If cornered, I suppose I myself would have had to admit to a predilection for thatched roofs and unevenly flagged floors. Ideally the garden would be thoroughly old-world. I could visualise myself sniffing at honeysuckle of a morning, possibly pruning apple trees and eradicating slugs from among the hollyhocks and delphiniums.

But I wasn't entirely free in the matter. One of the reasons for buying a cottage in the country had been to house an old friend who was deep in financial trouble. He was no longer young and at his best he had never been outstandingly skilled in dealing with practical problems. Knowing him as I did, I fancied that the minute he stepped on an unevenly flagged floor he would break an ankle. I questioned, too, whether he could manage to draw water from an old-world well, light old-world kerosene lamps or cope with leaks in an old-world thatched roof. That meant finding somewhere equipped with electricity, central heating, running water, a bathroom.

These things could be found easily enough, of course, in any provincial town; only there didn't seem much point in going from one agglomeration to another. Besides, except for places like Marseilles and Toulon, provincial towns tended to lose a good deal of their appeal from about eight o'clock in the evening. Thereafter, you had your choice between drinking glumly with travelling salesmen in the one café which stayed open until ten or staying at home and playing patience. On top of that, it could be taken for granted that the neophiles, once they had worked off their grudge against Paris, would move in on the provincial towns.

But the chances of finding something in the country with central heating and the rest of the modern conveniences were—well, chancy. When I first started hunting for a place, such gadgets were virtually unknown outside the cities. I inspected dozens of houses. They were as picturesque as anybody could want. Some of them also had electricity; but that was a bit too picturesque. It had clearly been installed by the local blacksmith after an imperfectly understood reading of a do-it-yourself manual. I had horrific visions of the garlands of naked wire coming into contact and the whole place bursting into flames. Other houses boasted running water. That is to say, the owners boasted of it. They seemed to feel that the sight of a dripping tap would convince me to close the deal on the spot. Only where there was running water there was no electricity and vice versa. And none of the places I saw possessed either central heating or a bathroom.

The house I finally located and bought had all the facilities I'd been looking for. Apart from that it was a distinct let-down in my estimation although the Parisian neophiles wouldn't have found a thing to object to. It was an uncompromisingly modern bungalow, the only building for miles around less than a hundred years old. Certain features of its construction suggested that it had been designed by an exhausted Soviet functionary in the employment of Gosplan. The windows on the first floor, for instance, suffered from a fairly basic defect which would have made any Muscovite feel right at home. They were traversed by heavy beams so that it was impossible to open them. Not that that was of any great importance since the lunatic architect had omitted to put in a staircase. Access to the upper storey could only be effected by oozing through a hatch in the ceiling and scrambling over wooden slats bestrewn with broken bottles left behind by the builders.

About all that could be said in mitigation was that the wretched place was unpretentious although an effort had been made to overcome that drawback by painting the exterior bright red. At least, I told myself, struggling forlornly to find the silver lining, the electrical installation wasn't unduly frightening, the running water ran, there was central heating and a bathroom with a bath in it. There were only six rooms but, as I learnt later on, my neighbours, awed by the central heating and the electricity, referred to it with no more than a touch of irony as 'the chateau'.

It was too bad about the old-world garden in which I'd proposed to play the squire. The chateau stood, arrogantly, in the middle of a paddock. You waded through glutinous mire to reach the door. Not a single hollyhock or honeysuckle was there to be sniffed. Anyone wanting to sniff rank grass and unidentifiable weeds, however, would have been in for a treat.

There were compensations—first and foremost, although I didn't realise it at the time, my immediate neighbours. With every one of them I was to form an enduring friendship. Then there was the setting. By sheer good luck I had come to the ancient province of the Berry in the Loire Valley. Vines covered the surrounding hills from horizon to horizon because, again by pure chance, I had picked a wine-growing region. It was not one of the illustrious regions that made oenophiles lift up their eyes in reverent gratitude, although over the years it was to acquire considerable renown, but it was nonetheless a wine-growing region and that in itself made up for a lot. The house, moreover, was situated not in a village but in what the French call a *lieu-dit*, a 'place-known-as' whatever it might be; and that was another advantage. I didn't share the conviction held by some foreigners that French peasants leaped at any opportunity to rob, and if possible, murder intruders. I was more concerned with the peasants' welfare than my own. They would appreciate it, I thought, if I wasn't in too close proximity. In a *lieu-dit* I could keep out of their way.

A 'place-known-as' is smaller than any village—a hamlet, I suppose, would be the nearest English equivalent. There are thousands of such minute communities in France. No doubt they appear on the army ordnance maps which show absolutely everything, from tool sheds down to sparrows' nests. They certainly won't figure on ordinary tourist maps, no matter how large the scale. Driving along a road you won't catch a glimpse of them. They are hidden from the outside world, reached as a rule by tortuous tracks. Ten miles away you ask in vain for directions to this one or that. Nobody will have heard of it.

The *lieu-dit* where I settled had no shops or cafés—not many *lieux-dit* do. It consisted of five or six houses, decent old grey houses which made my scarlet monstrosity look more offensive than ever. They were not aligned by the roadside but were tumbled together at random, either abutting on each other or separated by meandering paths. They had been occupied by the same families, all of them winegrowers, for generations past. When I arrived there in the early 1950s, there were no cars, no tractors, no telephones and, blessedly, no radios. Horses did the work of cars and tractors and local gossip conveyed any news just as rapidly and in much more detail than any radio.

Strictly speaking, I didn't in fact belong to this *lieu-dit*. It was on one side of a narrow dirt track, my house on the other. My old friend, my family and myself were the sole inhabitants of a separate 'place-known-as', one which was so obscure that nobody except the makers of the cadastral map were aware that there was such a place. A letter addressed to it would have baffled the postman. For the sake of convenience, therefore, we were informally regarded as residents of the hamlet across the way.

This private fief of mine was called Tayaux. Why the

'places-known-as' are known as what they are nobody can ever explain. Their names are invariably bizarre—Three Hedges (where there isn't one hedge, let alone three) or Black Castle (with no sign of a castle, black or white, in the vicinity) or The Hillside (probably lying in a featureless plain). One not far from me was called Le Gros Poisson. The Big Fish? It seemed improbable and when someone first mentioned it I thought the city slicker was being given a taste of rustic humour. But no, the place really existed. I would have been fascinated to learn how many centuries ago the big fish was caught, if he ever was caught (perhaps he owed his notoriety to the fact that no one ever succeeded in hooking him), and just how *gros* he really was. Any fish big enough to have a hamlet named after him must have been a whopper.

Tayaux itself was another mystery I would have liked to resolve but never did. Why Tayaux? A local historian came up with the suggestion that perhaps Tayaux was a corruption of *taïaut*!—tally-ho!—and since a neighbouring forest had always been plentifully stocked with deer and wild boar, the theory sounded plausible enough. But it was only a theory.

Like the hamlet on the other side of the road, Tayaux was, so to speak, a satellite of a village—in rural terms the equivalent of a major city—which was situated half-a-mile away. Its name could be roughly translated as 'The Smile in the Valley'. Parisian tourists were inclined to giggle at what they considered a sentimental and all too poetic designation. Furthermore, they took a supercilious view of the village itself. Rural villages were supposed to be picturesque, of course, but they saw this one, with its ancient houses grouped round an ancient church, with its communal well on the edge of a tiny square, with its blacksmith's forge, as a caricature, a postcard village. They would have preferred it to have at least one neon-lit drugstore or a glass pyramid or a façade composed of sewage pipes—all the things I was running away from.

No doubt the tourists would have jeered even more if they had known that there was a *sabotier* in the village, a maker of the *sabots* or wooden clogs that were once worn by children and adults alike. He looked like a duke—or at any rate he looked as those of us who don't know any imagine a duke should look. He had beautiful manners, the sort of manners, once again, that dukes ought to have. I met several old craftsmen like Monsieur Delaporte and every one of them, mysteriously, was of a distinguished appearance and spoke and behaved with striking courtesy.

Before the war, Monsieur Delaporte had fourteen employees working for him. They used to turn out I've forgotten how many pairs of sabots a day—a substantial number at all events. Now he had no employees and he himself only made an occasional pair as a favour. He made several pairs for my family and myself and after wearing them for a while we couldn't understand why they had been abandoned. Once we'd mastered the peculiar shuffle which was required if one was not to break one's leg, we were converted. Sabots kept one's feet warm in the bleakest weather, they were very much healthier than rubber or plastic boots and they lasted for ever. They were also eminently practical. After slogging through mud or snow, one kicked one's sabots off outside and entered the house in the felt slippers which were worn underneath, leaving the floors undirtied.

Calling on Monsieur Delaporte was always a pleasure. It was a fine sight, as one sipped the wine which he poured as soon as one arrived in his workshop, to see him delicately sculpting the inside of the sabot with his clasp knife until he'd achieved a perfect fit. He charged ridiculously little and would, I knew, have been happy to charge nothing whatever. But his innate courtesy made him realise that I would not have wanted to be given his beautiful creations for nothing. Only once did he insist on refusing payment. That was when he made a magnificent pair—out of walnut, the hardest wood to work—for my small daughter.

'They're wonderful, Monsieur Delaporte. My daughter will be enchanted. Now, please, what do I owe you?'

'Ah, Monsieur, not this time, I beg. You don't think I'd let you pay for these sabots? Your lovely little daughter—it's been a pleasure to make them for her.'

Monsieur Vattan was almost equally open-handed. He was one of the two carpenters in the village. The other was Monsieur Bizet whose family had been carpenters from father to son since the seventeenth century. I was sceptical when he told me this and rather meanly looked up the records in the village hall. They substantiated his claim as I should have known they would. I was properly impressed but, perhaps on account of his distinguished lineage, Monsieur Bizet's prices were somewhat higher than those of Monsieur Vattan. When it came to furnishing my house I chose Monsieur Vattan.

It was the right choice. His work may not have been quite as finished as that of Monsieur Bizet but this was compensated for by his singular reluctance to present his modest bills. His attitude towards money was like that of an 1890s aesthete. He came close to wincing fastidiously whenever the matter was raised.

The first thing he made for us was a table—solid oak without a screw or a nail in it—for a price agreed on in advance, and a very reasonable price at that. Shortly after it was delivered, I went to call on him.

'Good morning, Monsieur Vattan. I've come to settle my debts.'

'Ah, but Monsieur, I haven't had time to make out my bill.'

'That's of no importance, Monsieur Vattan. We agreed on the price, I think?'

'Of course, of course, Monsieur. But you must have the bill first. We must be businesslike, *n'est-ce pas?*'

'I assure you I don't need a bill, Monsieur Vattan. Nor a receipt. I have the cash here.'

'Some other time, Monsieur, some other time—when I've made out the bill. *Tiens*, eleven o'clock. What do you say to a glass of wine?'

Over the next twelve months or more, I made regular calls on Monsieur Vattan, imploring him to take the money I owed him. They always finished up the same way, with Monsieur Vattan leading me firmly to his cellar, the debt still unpaid. At first, I suspected some underhand scheme whereby I was to be charged twice as much as the agreed price. Paris friends had assured me that this was to be expected from the slippery avaricious folk in the country. But no, Monsieur Vattan's good faith was evident. After a while, I no longer anticipated that he would ever accept payment. My visits became a formality more than anything else.

'About that money I've owed you for so long, Monsieur Vattan . . . '

'Some other time, *cher Monsieur*. When I've made out the bill. I've been kept very busy lately. You haven't tried the new wine, have you?'

Off we went to the cellar.

In the end, with every sign of distaste, he did permit me to pay up. I couldn't help being a little irked when this happened. I'd come to think of Monsieur Vattan as being altogether detached from such coarse considerations as money. My consolation was that the trivial amount I eventually handed across and which he received with unconcealed revulsion could barely have covered the cost of the wine which I had been given.

A butcher's shop, a bakery and a little general store made up the shopping facilities in the village. That was enough for us. We had no hankering for *foie gras* or orchids or imported cigarettes. Anyway, you went to the shops not just to buy a leg of lamb or a kilo of potatoes but to pass the time of day. Shopping was largely a social event. Every now and again, the commercial transaction would be accompanied by a glass of wine. Professional *vignerons* or not, most people had a few vines of their own and made a certain quantity of wine. A glass was offered almost as ritually as coffee or mint tea among Turks and Arabs. After all, there was no hurry. That was a recognised fact of life. Instead of a terse demand and a surly reply as in Paris shops, there had to be a little conversation unconnected with the business of buying and selling. Usually this would have to do with some fearful disease or mishap of which a cousin or aunt had been a victim. Waiting customers showed no sign of impatience as the symptoms were described.

They knew the rules and were looking forward to having their turn. Before long I took to indulging in these medical discussions myself.

'You seem a trifle pale this morning, Monsieur.'

'Very possibly. I nearly stepped on a large adder a moment ago.'

'Let me tell you something, *cher Monsieur*. There are worse things than adders. Hornets. My Uncle Jules was stung by a hornet in 1940. It didn't seem to do him any harm but only six years later he was dead. Another three months and he would have been ninety-two. The hornet had sapped his strength, you see. *C'est pour vous dire.*'

'Perhaps he wasn't given the right treatment.'

'Ah, but he was, *cher Monsieur*. A hot poultice of willow leaves and spring onions macerated in red wine. There's no better treatment for hornet stings . . . '

Two elderly ladies, relics of deceased wine-growers, ran the general store. They greeted one cordially and were desolated when unable to supply some outlandish product never before requested—spaghetti, say, or a tin of sweetcorn. Once when I wanted some peanut butter for my children, they were at first incredulous and then aghast. Butter? Made out of peanuts, you say? And you eat it? No, that could not be. Heavens, what would such a concoction do to your stomach!

The baker was a good baker. He was at work from four in the morning every morning. Two hours later he would emerge, ghost-like in a film of flour, and be ready to serve. His oven was wood-burning. Impossible, he told me, to make edible bread any other way. Think of eating bread stinking of gas or either charred or soggy because you'd used electricity to cook with. He knew what he was talking about to judge from the quality of his bread. I'd never tasted better.

Ordinarily, I didn't much care for butchers' shops. A perfectly prepared *tournedos Rossini* or a *paupiette de veau* was one thing, chunks of bloody flesh and piles of innards were another. But Monsieur Boin's place was different. Le Petit Louis would probably have been critical but my own untutored opinion was that the quality of Monsieur Boin's meat was irreproachable. It was not that, however, which set his shop apart. For him, the selling of meat was only a sideline. His heart, you might say, was not in the blood-bespattered shop but in the room behind it. This was a café although it resembled a salon rather than a saloon. The Jockey Club in Paris had the reputation of being savagely exclusive. Needless to say, I had never tried to force my way in but I was ready to bet it wasn't half as choosy as Monsieur Boin's place.

Since it was an officially licensed café customers could not be refused admittance. But if they didn't look like the right sort of people they were at once humiliated, spiritually blackballed, psychologically snubbed. A fat chance they had of getting a drink *chez Boin!*

Those of us who were members in good standing had a part to play in excluding undesirables. Some objectionably powerful car would draw up. A brace of self-assured Parisians would come in with the amused air of socialites on a tour of the slums. We got to work. Conversation would have been animated and frequently passionate up until then ('*Non, mais dis donc*, are you trying to tell *me* how to filter wine?') but it came to a sudden and menacing stop as soon as the interlopers entered. Sometimes the effect was so overpowering that they would turn right round and go out again. If they had the courage to remain we would stare silently at them. If they still persisted, Monsieur Boin himself would deal with them.

'Wine? *Mon pauvre Monsieur*, the last barrel has turned sour. What are the others drinking? Oh, they'll drink anything, sour or not—they don't know the difference. They're just roughnecks. But I couldn't offer it to you and your lady. It'd give you the colic. Beer? Not a drop. Ah, you can't rely on anyone nowadays. I've been waiting for a delivery for weeks.'

'Well, let us have two coffees.'

'If only I could! The coffee machine broke down just forty-eight hours ago. *Que voulez-vous?* It's as I say, you can't rely on anybody or anything. Machines break down almost as soon as you've bought them and of course the repairman is always too busy to come and fix them. What a world, Monsieur, what a world!'

'So what can you give us?'

'Nothing, *mon pauvre Monsieur*, nothing at all. Ah, things were different before the war. But I'll tell you. Twenty kilometres further on—The Three Ponds. There's a café there. I don't know how the *patron* does it but he's never short of anything. Mind you, his wife is *very* friendly with the Prefect.'

Then, once the parched Parisians had gone, 'Drink up, *mes enfants*, this is my round.'

There was another café in the village, presided over by 'La Rose'. She was prodigiously aged, prodigiously amiable, prodigiously garrulous and prodigiously indifferent to money. A drink *chez La Rose* was the equivalent of about six anywhere else. You paid for your first drink and thereafter, as soon as you took a swig from your glass, La Rose would fill it up again. Glasses that weren't filled, really filled, distressed her. You might decide you'd had enough. La Rose never thought so.

'*Allons*, Monsieur, a little wine never hurt anyone. *Bien au contraire*. Take the case of my poor brother, Arsène. Bronchitis, that's what it was, and the doctor said it would turn into pneumonia. Ah, these doctors! To listen to them you'd think we were all going to drop dead in five minutes. This one gave my poor brother enough medicine to drown a cat in. Arsène poured the whole lot down the sink, every last drop. He knew what he was doing, Arsène. Science is all very well but we know a thing or two that these doctors don't. What do you think he did, my poor Arsène? He drank five bottles of red wine every day instead of his usual three. Then before going to sleep he drank two big glasses of *marc*. He never did get pneumonia and in a week he was up and about and as spry as ever. *Ce pauvre imbécile de médecin* thought it was thanks to his tablets and tonics, can you believe it? You just finish your glass, Monsieur, and let me fill it up for you.'

CHAPTER EIGHT

All this was in the future. I received the same austere reception as any other interloper the first few times I sidled into Monsieur Boin's back room. La Rose didn't take me to her heart the instant she glimpsed me. Months went by before I felt sufficiently sure of myself to join in the head-shaking discussions of Monsieur Machin's sciatica or Madame Untel's dropsy.

No banners were hung out when I arrived in the hamlet but then I wasn't expecting any public display of enthusiasm. On the other hand, I wasn't attacked by resentful peasants with scythes and pikes, either. Nobody made a sign to ward off the evil eye when I passed by. That was good enough for me. Anything short of outright hatred could be taken as tantamount to being given a rousing welcome.

Back then the old peasant traditions were very much as they had been for centuries past. Wariness when confronted with strangers was one of them. My nearest neighbour, Maxime, was decidely warier than the others. He carried caution to the point of systematically refusing to say yes or no to any proposition of whatever kind. '*C'est possible*' was as far as he was prepared to go.

A week or so after I settled in I needed to ask him something or other. Like everyone else for several miles around, he of course knew who I was, how much I'd paid for the house, how long I'd lived in France, what I did for a living, my age—everything down to my height and the colour of my hair. When you intrude on a small rural community you'd better give up any thought of preserving your anonymity for longer than fifteen minutes. I was certain that my impending arrival had been abundantly commented on and that the comments had been compounded of equal doses of curiosity and apprehension.

None of this was apparent in Maxime's reception of me. As a matter of principle, he was not going to let on that he had ever heard of my existence. Alerted by barking dogs, he planted himself on the doorstep of his house and watched me approach with Cherokee impassivity. I did my best to look at ease.

'*Bonjour, Monsieur.* My name is Kershaw.'

Dead silence followed this while Maxime thought over what I had said. Having made his mind up, he eyed me unwaveringly and gave me his considered opinion of this claim.

'*C'est possible.*'

Everyone in the hamlet knew about this idiosyncrasy of Maxime's and nobody paid any attention to it. It was understood that he would never in any circumstances commit himself. He might be standing under a torrential rainstorm but if I or anyone else happened to remark, '*Tiens*, this really is heavy rain,' Maxime, inscrutable as ever, would brood over the assertion and then, with water streaming down his face, would concede, '*C'est possible.*'

When I had got to know him, when we were good friends and I felt I could permit myself the liberty, I would try, just for the fun of it, to badger him into being less noncommittal. It was a waste of time. Maxime wasn't going to allow some misbegotten Australian to change the habit of a lifetime.

'What about a glass or two of wine, Maxime? It's my birthday.'

'*C'est possible.*'

'Listen, Maxime, it isn't merely possible, it isn't merely probable either, it's not a matter of conjecture or guesswork, it's the plain truth, damn it. I tell you it's my birthday and you may as well accept it.'

'*C'est possible.*'

Coming up against this inflexible '*C'est possible*' for the first time was all the more unnerving because the implied scepticism concerned my name. I'd heard about identity crises but I'd never experienced one before. With a single laconic phrase Maxime threw me off balance. I felt as though I'd been caught using an alibi. Or could it be, I wondered agitatedly, that I was suffering from some dark hallucination? Perhaps my name was not Kershaw, as I'd always believed. In which case, who was I, what was I?

As time went by it was accepted by Maxime and everyone else that I really was called Kershaw, unlikely as it might seem. Nonetheless my name continued to cause difficulties. It had been bad enough in Paris where people were more or less accustomed to encountering barbarous foreign names; here it was much worse. It was well known that there were no k's or w's in the French language. A name which began with one and ended with the other was enough to make anyone suspicious. And the h in the middle could not, by all the laws of God and the French Academy, be preceded by an s. Until we adopted more easy-going forms of address, my neighbours assailed me with all sorts of fugal variations on Kershaw: Kharkov, Kazakh, Kirghiz, Khiva and Kvass were just a few of them. I was always expecting somebody, without meaning any harm, to come out with Monsieur Khruschchev or—why not?—Monsieur Krishnamurti but, in the event, the worst that happened to me was to be greeted on one occasion as Monsieur Karloff and on another as Monsieur Kafka.

It was no surprise to anyone that such a preposterous name should be accompanied by an equally preposterous nationality. Australian—what next! Foreigners were not popular. And virtually everyone was a foreigner. Inhabitants of hamlets no more than a few hundred metres away were foreigners. So, in particular, were Parisians. The rare specimens who passed through the district were received, if they were received at all, with every sign of aversion. They were felt to have a condescending attitude towards country folk—which was generally true although three-quarters of them had most likely only emigrated to the capital themselves ten or fifteen years earlier. All Parisians were assumed to be spies in the pay of the taxation authorities or something worse. If there was anything worse.

Paris, moreover, was the symbol of the Revolution and the

countless vexations that had resulted. The Revolution was the source of all evils from the centralisation of power to mildew and drought. When you asked a French peasant where he was born or where So-and-so lived he would never refer to the '*départements*' created by the Revolution but to the old provinces which officially no longer existed. One of the earliest of my blunders was when I casually remarked to a neighbour, 'Here in the Cher . . . '

Eyeing me balefully he put me in my place, figuratively and literally. '*You* may be in the Cher, Monsieur, *we* are in the Berry.'

In some ways, being Australian was the ideal nationality. During the Occupation a small number of German soldiers had been stationed nearby. Otherwise, not a soul in the neighbourhood had ever seen a foreigner—neither an Englishman nor an American, let alone a Pole, a Greek, a Swede, a Russian, a Swiss or a citizen of any other country than France. But there was no getting away from the fact that the brutes were close at hand and it was taken for granted that they were exactly the same as Germans, that they represented the same menace, that they were determined as soon as they got the chance to invade France and spread fire and rapine.

Australians were not felt to pose any such threat for the simple reason that nobody had ever heard of us. We enjoyed about as much notoriety as Pitcairn Islanders. I can't remember whether I mentioned my nationality to Maxime when we first met. If I did he certainly received the information with a dubious '*C'est possible.*' A handful of octogenarians had fought in the 1914–18 war and had some recollection of '*les Anzacs*' but as to where these Anzacs had come from, unless from a remote land called Anzacia, they were unable to say. An exceptionally bright lad in the village school assured me that he knew about Australia. He even knew that it was an island. Somewhere in the Caribbean, he rather thought.

The bright lad wasn't by any means the only one who was unsure of the whereabouts of my native land. I had had to go to Paris for the space of a weekend. By this time I had got past the stage where my neighbours and I limited our social exchanges to a mechanical '*Bonjour*'. On my return I was amiably questioned as to what I had been up to for the last forty-eight hours. So how had I found things in Australia? Father and mother well? Aunts and uncles and cousins, too? When it was discovered that I had spent the whole time in Paris the reaction was one of rather disapproving astonishment. With forty-eight hours to spare I could surely have whipped over to Australia, possibly between lunch at the Coupole and dinner at the Closerie des Lilas. It was all too clear what everyone was thinking. An odd lot, these foreigners—no feeling for family ties whatever.

The lack of family sentiment attributed to me was offset to some extent by my curiosity value. Frenchmen from anywhere but the Berry were only minimally better than Italians or Portuguese. My nationality put me into a separate unique category. As an Australian, I became an object of interest, an inoffensive freak midway between a village idiot and a two-headed calf. If there had been any tourists around in those days I would have been a tourist attraction, probably listed in the guidebooks as 'worth a detour'. Compared to me, the numerous chateaux throughout the region wouldn't have been on any tourist's itinerary. The situation suited me perfectly. Far from objecting to the half-incredulous scrutiny to which I was subjected when I announced my nationality, I considered myself fortunate. Better to be a two-headed calf any day than a Greek or a Swiss plotting to lay the country waste.

It wasn't only my nationality which made me into what was known as the '*loup blanc*', the white wolf, the oddity of the district. The eccentric way I dressed would have been enough by itself to set me apart. My clothes, especially in summer when I wore thin cotton trousers, a short-sleeved shirt and sandals, provoked a combination of amazement and compassion. 'Did you see our Australian wandering around practically naked today? *Mon vieux*, what a get-up! It's a miracle that he hasn't died of pneumonia!'

Normal peasant garb in those days consisted of corduroy trousers, a flannel vest, a thick shirt (sometimes two in inclement weather), a sweater, a waistcoat and a jacket. Berets were worn by some of the ancients but the usual headgear was a cloth cap which was never removed indoors or out. Should the temperature drop below 25°C, a cumberbund might be added together with a scarf twisted several times round the neck. When the heat became unendurable—more than 30°C— it was considered permissible, although a trifle foolhardy, to dispense with the scarf.

Then there was my exotic French. I had a foreign accent, I knew, but no one in Paris guffawed or fell back when I opened my mouth. In my adopted hamlet, it was not unusual for people to suppose that I was speaking some strange Australian dialect. Their puzzlement was nothing compared to mine. The local *patois* transformed '*Qu'est-ce qu'ils ont dit?*' into '*Kee-kee-zon-dee?*' and '*Tu feras bien ce que tu voudras*' into '*Tu frar ban sker tu voora*'. All sorts of words which didn't figure in any dictionary provided an additional complication. How was I to guess that a *babiot* was a robin redbreast or that to be *empicassé* meant to be bewitched? How was I to guess that a whole string of standard French words had acquired quite different meanings on arriving in the Berry? *Brave*, I eventually understood, did not signify courageous, as I'd supposed, but handsome and a *poëllée* was not a panful as it would have been in Paris but a feast.

There were innumerable traps and I fell into the lot, one after another. The first time I overheard a reference to Bertillon I was surprised and impressed that the topic should interest two wine-growers. By way of showing that Australians knew just as much as Berrichons, I chipped in with what I thought was a pretty shrewd comment on my own account. It turned out, though, that it was not the inventor of anthropometry they were discussing; a *bertillon* was the Berrichon term for a vine branch. And there were a number of embarrassing misunderstandings before it was explained to me that *cocu* was not used in a spirit of ribaldry; it designated a resinous substance exuded by cherry trees.

With the detestable facility of children, my son and daughter had mastered the *patois* while I was still mixing up *queriotte* (a small stone) with *querlotte* (a pot for boiling water). You tend to make a fool of yourself when you ask for a small stone in which to boil some water or remark that the field is covered with pots. I never did become fluent, even approximately fluent, in Berrichon but I made enough progress to survive. In fact, I did more than merely survive. On one unforgettable occasion I, the two-headed calf, actually inflicted a linguistic humiliation on two Frenchmen.

A friend from Marseilles had come to spend a week with us. I had lived for a while in the South and was accustomed to the meridional accent. By then, too, I had a fair understanding of the Berrichon *patois*. I took Edouard over to Maxime's cellar for a glass of wine.

They exchanged greetings with no difficulty. Then Maxime said something or other. Edouard looked at me with frank incomprehension, smiled miserably and remained silent.

'*Kee-kee-la?*' Maxime asked. I knew enough to interpret this as '*Qu'est-ce qu'il a?*'

'He wonders what's the matter with you,' I told Edouard.

'I can't understand a word he says, that's what's the matter.'

'Well, say something, for God's sake.'

Edouard muttered that he was delighted to be visiting the Berry or some equally idiotic commonplace. In his nervousness, his powerful southern accent became even more pronounced.

'*Non, mais,*' snapped Maxime. 'Who is this *godais?*'

'Maxime thinks you must be half-witted,' I explained to Edouard.

'He does? Well, tell him I think *he's* half-witted. Why can't he talk like everyone else?'

I translated for Maxime. 'That's what I was wondering about *him*. Who is he? Another damned Australian, I suppose.'

'He's as French as you are.'

'*C'est possible,*' said Maxime but I could see he didn't believe it for an instant.

More than anything else, what set me apart, of course, was the fact that I wasn't a peasant. Everybody else in the hamlet was. Not to be a peasant in Australia would have been something to brag about. I remembered the pub disputes which used to end with the ultimate put-down, 'Ah, you bloody peasant!' It was much the same in Paris. Most of the recurring brawls between motorists would culminate in the drivers scornfully dismissing each other as *pauvres péquenots, pauvres paysans.*

Where I was now living there was nothing derogatory about the word peasant. Very much the reverse. Peasants were proud of being peasants. '*Nous les paysans . . .* ' my neighbours would say with a note of superiority in their voices. For them, 'city-dweller' was as contemptuous a term as 'peasant' for Parisians—or Australians.

I could never decide just what it was that distinguished a peasant from an agriculturist, a grazier, a farmer. All I knew was that I had been brought into contact with another race. That pride bordering on self-satisfaction had something to do with it, no doubt. An Australian farmer might enjoy being a farmer; he would hardly exult in it. If everything was going well with him he might be sorry for city-dwellers sweating out their lives in offices or factories. He would not look down on them as a sub-species—or, if he did, he would keep his opinion to himself.

Continuity came into it, too. A farmer might be the second or third generation to work the land. In my part of the Berry, not many peasants could tell you for how many generations their families had lived in the same houses, cultivated the same fields. They had an atavistic attachment to the soil. It was part of them and they were part of it.

Consanguinity was another element. Everybody was more or less distantly related to everybody else. They mightn't be quite sure whether So-and-so was a second or third cousin or simply the aunt by marriage of a cousin twice removed but they were all related in one way or another.

It should have made for a population of enfeebled morons.

Somehow, it hadn't. All the peasants I ever came across were intimidatingly stalwart physical specimens. I would have hated to get into a fight with any of them. They might never have read a book in their lives—I knew quite a lot who would have had trouble doing so if they had wanted to—but they were no less intelligent because of it. I had met plenty of intellectuals who were a good deal stupider. In fact, lumbered with absurd theories practically *all* the intellectuals I'd come across were stupider. Peasants thought for themselves. They didn't wait to get an authorisation from the current swami before making up their minds.

None of the stereotypes fitted, I came to realise. Where was he, that surly French peasant, forever on the verge of flying into a homicidal tantrum and screaming imprecations? Perhaps he was lurking around in other parts of the country but I never encountered him. It was positively disappointing to meet with consistent affability and a permanent readiness to render a service. The authors of realistic earthy novels from whom I'd derived my preconceptions had let me down.

They had let me down in other respects, too. As far as I ever saw, none of my neighbours spent their evenings slavering over an accumulation of gold. They didn't waste money—at that time, they had very little to waste—and they would have thought anyone who did an imbecile. I imagine they would have wanted pretty solid guarantees before making a cash loan to a persuasive businessman. But if we ourselves ran out of butter or milk we could always borrow from someone in the hamlet and any attempt to return whatever it might be was taken as an affront. I never took up the invitations to help myself from their gardens but fruit and vegetables were periodically bestowed on us, unasked for.

It was not long before I realised that I myself would never be able to write the sort of realistic earthy novel that made urban readers feel so pleasantly superior. If you want to write novels like that the important thing is not to know what you're talking about.

CHAPTER NINE

I began to make friends. It was a lengthy business. In Paris, you'd get into conversation with somebody in a café, find him congenial and within an hour the two of you would be on first-name terms. That was how I got to know Alain and a lot of other mad wags at the Coupole. It wasn't like that in the country. From the very outset, relations with the inhabitants of the hamlet had been correct, pleasant even, but not exactly effusive. I had to be examined from a distance, sized up. Any effort to hurry things along I knew would be a blunder. It was not for me, the white wolf, to determine when and how my position in the neighbourhood should be modified. A cautious advance was essential, with an eye kept open for ambushes. I was no Freemason (if I had been, it would have been the end of me in a firmly Catholic community) but I saw my initiation into the everyday life of the hamlet as something like a Freemason's slow ascent through the successive grades of his craft. Masons could only rise in the hierarchy, I'd been told, after undergoing a series of esoteric tests and ordeals. Tests and ordeals were just what I was called on to undergo.

Unpredictably, it was the stony-faced Maxime who conducted me step by step as I strove to become the rustic equivalent of a Grand Master. For several months, like the others, he had contented himself with a perfunctory '*Bonjour*' when we happened to meet. One day, suddenly and startlingly, instead of marching ahead, he stopped, looked me over for a moment while I wondered what on earth I could have done wrong and then, his expression as discouraging as ever, he growled, 'I'm going to have a glass of wine. Come on, if you want one, too.'

He sounded as if it didn't matter to him whether I came along or not and, in fact, as though he were already regretting that he'd proposed it. But this was no time for me to be touchy. Extended by a member of the guild of winegrowers, the invitation was the Legion of Honour, the Prix Goncourt, election to the Senate, a seat in the Académie Française. Shopkeepers and craftsmen offered a glass of wine more or less as a matter of course. No special distinction was implied by the gesture. To be invited to the cellar of a winegrower was very different and highly significant. Only fellow *vignerons* and especially favoured acquaintances were admitted to the privilege. As long as I didn't commit some appalling solecism, I was on the way to becoming a recognised member of decent society.

Maxime remained his taciturn self as we descended to the cellar. Without a word, he filled a glass. One glass only, because there was no other. Of spectacular capacity—it must have held close to half-a-litre—it was further remarkable by reason of its form. Instead of having a foot to it, the stem tapered to a point. Hence you could only dispose of it by first emptying it of its considerable contents and then placing it somewhere upside down or handing it to the next drinker. Very often, to make the procedure still more daunting, there would be half-a-dozen of us in Maxime's cellar. With everyone waiting for a go at the solitary glass, politeness demanded that you should do your best to consume the whole half-litre or whatever it was in one heroic gulp.

Still preserving an unbroken and intimidating silence, Maxime watched me drink. When I had emptied the great cyclopean vessel, he refilled it and drained it without once removing it from his lips. Then he filled it again and, wordlessly, handed it across. Each of us swallowed three glasses. At no point did either of us speak. I sensed that I was being subjected to one of those Masonic tests or ordeals. After the third glass had been emptied, Maxime signified that the party was over by grunting, 'I must get back to work.' I didn't get back to work myself. I spent the rest of the afternoon in a stupor.

Three or four days after this preliminary rite, I received what

I took to be a signal that I hadn't done all that badly. At least, this seemed to be implied by the fact that I was once again invited to the cellar. Once again Maxime saluted me curtly, once again he scrutinised me at length, once again (and once again sounding as though he were by no means sure he was doing the right thing) he grumblingly invited me to have a drink. There was, however, a marked and auspicious change in his behaviour. In the cellar, to my astonishment, he became positively loquacious. He must have uttered fully a dozen sentences. His impenetrable Berrichon accent prevented me from following what he was talking about with any certainty but the important thing was that he had spoken and, as far as I could judge, spoken in cordial tones. From time to time, I thought I had understood something and then I ventured a '*Tiens*' or a '*Ça alors*'. I also used an ingenious technique which was to come in useful on a number of occasions and which consisted of articulating an unidentifiable noise I'd devised. It could be taken to mean either '*oui*' or '*non*' as the context demanded. As I became more expert I could when necessary give it a twist which enabled the other party to interpret it, according to choice, as 'I've never heard anything so outrageous' or 'What will they think of next?'

Despite the progress I'd clearly made in Maxime's esteem, I knew that my induction was not yet complete. Even though it soon became a regular thing for Maxime and me to empty that colossal glass of his whenever we bumped into each other, a long and hazardous path lay ahead. Several months elapsed before I was at last received into the fraternity by being baptised.

Baptism as practised by the winegrowers of the district was not as canonical as might be thought. No period of instruction was provided for. What happened was that a decision would be reached (I never found out what the criteria were) that the time had come for So-and-so to be baptised. I was a bit disquieted when Maxime informed me with a villainous grin that it was my turn. If I was expected to submit to total immersion in wine, I wasn't ready for it. Maxime reassured me. The candidate was merely required to kneel (that was the only religious aspect of the proceedings) amid a circle of witnesses. Using a glass pipette for the purpose, the officiating *vigneron* then drew an alarming quantity of wine from the cask. The candidate threw back his head, opened his mouth, the *vigneron* removed his thumb from the end of the pipette and an uninterrupted jet of wine was shot down the postulant's throat. Spilling a single drop nullified the ceremony and provoked cries of contempt and derision from the onlookers. I did well enough to avoid being hooted although a couple of times while frantically swallowing I thought I might have to push the pipette to one side.

Our friend Françoise did better than I did, a lot better. My performance had been average, hers was epic. Always unashamedly susceptible where pretty young women were concerned, Maxime decreed early on that Françoise merited baptism. Much as I loved her, I was piqued. Why should this honour be bestowed on her? She was only a visitor, a frequent and welcome visitor, but still no more than a visitor. When I thought how long I, a resident, had had to wait . . .

Maxime knew what he was doing, though. Françoise drank down the wine as though it had been milk, not that milk would have been all that easy to swallow if served from a pipette. With a bravado I found hard to forgive, she then insisted that the ceremony be repeated, this time with a potent *marc* replacing the wine. Exclamations of admiration mingled with perturbation burst forth from the assembly. '*Cette pauv' petite dame*, she's going to kill herself!' Nothing of the kind. The poor little lady was not that easy to kill. Getting on her knees again, she threw back her head and opened her mouth. Maxime aimed the pipette. Down went the incandescent spirit on top of the wine. Looking like Joan of Arc, Françoise rose to her feet. She didn't even waver. No comparable feat had been brought off within the memory of the oldest *vigneron* present.

In spite of my baptism, Maxime and I continued to address each other as 'Monsieur', scrupulously using the second person plural. Heaven knows how long we might have continued to behave like a pair of eighteenth-century exquisites if it had not been for my impossible name. Against all probability, it actually turned out to be an asset. Desperately grappling one day with 'Kershaw', Maxime suddenly gave way to a spasm of exasperation. 'Kossoff, Kishav, Ketchow—how do you expect anybody to pronounce a name like that?' and, slightly varying his usual formula, '*C'est pas possible*! What's your first name—something even worse, I suppose?'

'Alister.'

'Alistairre. That's another heathen name, if ever I heard one. But at least I can say it. Alistairre, Alistairre. *Bon*, from now on I'll call you Monsieur Alistairre. You'd better call me Maxime.'

'Then you'd better call me Alistairre—without any Monsieur.'

'*Bon, bon*, Maxime, Alistairre—agreed.'

We clinked glasses.

I went home feeling jubilant. To have got onto these terms with a French peasant, particularly in those days and particularly for a foreigner and particularly if the foreigner happened to be an Australian—that was something out of the ordinary. When I became chummy with the count in the sixteenth *arrondissement*, he had never suggested that I should call him by his first name but I only knew him for some two months. A week or so more and we would certainly have been Maximilien and Alister to each other. It had taken well over a year to reach the same degree of intimacy with Maxime. We respected the proprieties in the country.

Now that Maxime, a recognised arbiter in such matters, had given the lead, there was a fair chance that his example would be followed by the rest of my neighbours. It was. Not immediately, of course. For some time, Maxime reserved to himself the right to address me as plain Alistairre. Others who ventured to adopt the same familiarity got a dirty look from him. For everyone except Maxime I remained *Monsieur* Alistairre. All the same, there was no question about it—I was ascending more and more swiftly through the Masonic degrees.

Already an Entered Apprentice I very soon became a Fellow Craft and when Paul, another near neighbour, invited me to his lodge, it was clear that before long I would qualify as a Master Mason. Grand Mastership, which had once been only a dream, was now within my reach.

Right from the beginning Paul had been more forthcoming than Maxime. We now became, and remained, good friends. I had plenty of reasons to be glad of it. One of the many things about me that were a permanent source of disbelief was my inability to carry out the simplest manual task. Changing a light bulb strained my technological skills to the utmost. Paul could do anything and was ready to handle any difficulties which might confront me. In the end, I had only to arrive at his door looking harassed. He would glance at his wife Germaine with a look that clearly betokened, 'Here we go again—would you believe it?' Then, dropping whatever he was doing, he would prepare to cope with my latest problem.

Physically, Paul was of awe-inspiring stature and force. His son, Jean-Marc, was a child of two or three when I first knew him but already gave promise of becoming equally massive. He kept his promise. When still an adolescent, his hands were great bear paws and the circumference of his arms was roughly that of a telegraph pole. Once, when he was a very small boy, I threatened to box his ears for some misdemeanour or other. Only a short while afterwards, he could have boxed my ears and I would not have been fool enough to resist.

By the time he had reached that stage he derived the same innocent pleasure as his father in bringing home to me my pathetic clumsiness which he manifestly equated with total physical and possibly mental debility. Aged not more than fourteen, he watched me one day as I unhandily wielded a pickaxe in an effort to demolish a stone wall. An hour's work enabled me to dislodge a handful of pebbles. Sheer exhaustion and Jean-Marc's unblinking regard finally overcame me. I dropped the pickaxe and went off to have a drink at Monsieur Boin's. I was not gone for very long. When I got back, there was no more wall. Jean-Marc never subsequently alluded to the matter but from then on he smiled his father's amiably mocking smile whenever he saw me.

The incident gave me an idea which more than once was to prove very useful. I didn't need, I realised, to go around imploring someone to help me out. All I had to do was to wait until there was a witness and then set about trying to perform whatever task needed to be done even more unskilfully than was natural to me. Sooner or later, whoever might be watching, partly out of good nature and partly out of irritation at my bungling, would come and take over.

With Maxime I used a slightly different version of this method. Generally, he was as willing as anyone else to lend a hand. Sometimes, however, he would be too busy or in too bad a temper to rescue me. This was the case one day when, for some reason, I was trying to dig a hole. It suddenly occurred to me that I might get results if I were to proclaim that the task was not just beyond my powers but beyond anyone else's and specifically Maxime's. Passing the gate, he had stopped to have a little fun at my expense.

'Well, well, don't tell me the city boy is actually working?'

'Not too badly, either. I only started at eight o'clock this morning and I've dug down six centimetres already.'

'How deep have you got to go?'

'Two metres.'

'Two metres! At the rate you're going, you'll be lucky if you manage to dig one metre before St Vincent's Day.'

'I'd like to see anyone do better.'

'*Comment, comment!* I could dig down two metres in an hour and not even be out of breath.'

I took my cue.

'In an hour? It can't be done.'

'An hour, I tell you—maybe less.'

'It can't be done.'

'*Non, mais tu es fou?* In an hour, I tell you.'

'It can't be done.'

'Give me that shovel!'

Fooling around with a French peasant can be hazardous. As

soon as he'd had time to think it over, Maxime realised that I'd scored off him. He didn't accuse me openly. That wasn't his way. And he was in no hurry to get his own back. The locals were fond of quoting a proverb to the effect that revenge is a dish best eaten cold. Maxime agreed.

Some weeks went by. I had forgotten my little trick. Not Maxime. He called out to me as I was heading, as usual, for Monsieur Boin's.

'What about doing something to help me for a change?'

'Glad to, Maxime.'

'That's fine. You can give me a hand to get the hay in.'

Armed with a pitchfork, I was stationed in the loft. Similarly equipped, Maxime took his place on the cart below.

'Are you ready? All right, I'll fork the hay up to you and you fork it to the back of the loft.

Up came the hay. I forked away energetically. But not energetically enough. Maxime was sending up the stuff at a pace which I had no hope of matching. I was beginning to choke on the dust. A mound of hay steadily accumulated around me.

'Hey, Maxime, slow down, can't you? I'm up to my knees in your damned hay.'

'You can manage—just keep at it.'

I kept at it. The mound grew higher. It was up to my waist. I felt as though I were sinking into quicksand. I wasn't just querulous any longer, I was getting scared.

'Fork away, *mon petit Alistairre*.'

'I'm forking, damn it, but I won't be forking much longer, that's for sure. I'm being smothered. Will you please stop and let me out. I can't fork fast enough, I tell you.'

'You mean'—and I could hear the malevolent triumph in his voice—'You mean it can't be done?'

Our undeclared war was not over with this victory of Maxime's. Another battle was still to be fought. Providence rather than any strategic genius on my part enabled me to win it.

'Look at that sky, Maxime. It's going to rain buckets in a minute.'

Made by a fellow peasant, the remark wouldn't have elicited anything more than the customary, '*C'est possible*'. Coming from me, Maxime took it amiss. It was presumption on my part, an encroachment on his rural authority. He began a ferocious diatribe.

'*Tu me fais rire!* You don't know what you're talking about. How could you? You've lived all your life in cities—poor urbanite, poor street-sweeper, poor factory hand. Now we peasants—*nous autres paysans*—we know a thousand things that you don't, with all your books and measuring rods. *We* can tell what the weather's going to be like with no trouble at all. Just to give you an idea, if the ladybirds start flying around or if the donkeys roll in the dust or if the poppies have been drooping and begin to straighten up, then you can count on good weather. You didn't know that, did you? Now as to this famous rain of yours—you can tell it's going to rain if the chimney doesn't draw properly or if the cocks crow at night or if the bread gets damp. Well, is your chimney drawing badly, have you heard any cocks crowing at night, has your bread got damp? No! There you are, then. So it's not going to rain for weeks to come, maybe months—get that into your city-dweller's head. It's impossible for it to rain, you'll be lucky if you see a drop before . . . '

Precisely at that point it began to rain. It rained with a violence that no one in the district had ever experienced. I said nothing. To have allowed myself to jeer would have marred the beauty of the moment. I simply looked at Maxime, trying to make my features as rigid as his. It was a pleasure to watch his frustration as he struggled to think of something to say which would restore his position as a wise old peasant. Under that downpour, there was nothing to be said that could alleviate his discomposure. In the end, '*Merde!*' and he stalked off to his cellar.

'Aren't I invited, Maxime?'

'*Merde!*'

My children played a major part in bringing about my definitive integration. True, they both had the same ludicrous family name as I had, poor mites, but they were not responsible for that. Their first names, at least, were perfectly proper, Christian names in fact. Saint Sylvain was the patron saint of the Berry—that was my son's name. The patron saintess—or whatever the feminine of saint may be—was Solange, my daughter's name. The choice argued that I was not entirely devoid of good feeling.

Fluent in the *patois* (so that I had to beg them to revert to French when talking to me) they played with the local children, Jean-Marc among them, and were adopted by their friends' parents. They were popular with everybody and I benefited in consequence by a sort of ricochet effect.

As a rule, Maxime showed no great liking for the company of small children, but he made an exception in Sylvain's case. He was prone to horrendous outbursts of rage when anything went wrong and during these frightful tantrums everyone, including his own children, kept well out of his way. Sylvain alone displayed no sign of trepidation whatever.

We were given conclusive proof of Maxime's attachment to my son when he acquired a tractor, one of the first in the hamlet. It was a ramshackle contraption of indeterminate age and origin but it worked more or less adequately once it was started. The problem was to start it. Morning after morning, we would hear the engine rasping horribly and then a frenzied string of oaths from Maxime.

'*Bon sang de 'cré nom de putain de merde de bordel de saloperie . . .*'

This was the signal for everyone to get under cover. Not Sylvain. Approaching Maxime, whose veins by then would be dilated and whose face would be an apoplectic purple, Sylvain would inquire gently, 'Isn't it working, Maxime?' Maxime's arms would fly galvanically upwards. His hands would curve into a strangler's claws. That's the end of Sylvain, we would think sadly, watching from a safe distance. But incredibly, mastering his fury with an effort that was nothing short of preternatural, '*Eh, non, mon petit Sylvain*,' Maxime would reply, 'it's not working.' Then, as the engine for the twentieth time failed to respond to his demented winding of the starting handle, '*Boxon de garce de con de vache . . .* '

It all helped to enrich Sylvain's vocabulary. Mine, too.

Solange formed another tie with the hamlet through the unlikely medium of goats. The region was famous for its goat cheeses and every household had its flock of the animals. Every household likewise had a grandmother and the goats were the grandmother's responsibility. Both goats and grandmothers grew rarer as time went by. Whether the grandmothers died off because they no longer had goats to look after or whether the goats went into a decline because of the disappearance of the grandmothers I never knew.

They were a charming sight, the black-shawled and rheumatically contorted grandmothers, as they led their flocks off each morning to graze ('*moder*' in the local idiom) and led them back in the evening, strikingly reminiscent of an illustration in a mediaeval Book of Hours. All of them became Solange's grandmothers. She would bestow her company on each of them in turn. From the window I would see them setting off together across the fields, the infinitely ancient old lady and the small blonde girl. Reaching the chosen spot they would settle down, the goats to graze, the grandmother to knit and Solange to chatter.

I was also beginning to form agreeable relationships outside the hamlet. In one of the neighbouring villages there was a bistro which I came to cherish as in the past I had cherished the Coupole. More, perhaps, because not even the Coupole achieved the same degree of conviviality. It was the only bistro I ever encountered where the proprietors, Raymonde and Pascal, and favoured clients, myself among them, intermingled to the point of being almost indistinguishable. It was never clear who was serving or who was paying or whether we were dining at Raymonde's and Pascal's table or they at ours.

In this uniquely sociable establishment conversations would spontaneously occur even between complete strangers who, after a few glasses of wine had been exchanged, would cease to be strangers. It was in this way that I met another Pascal and his father, Marcel, proprietors of one of the largest and most highly reputed vineyards in the district. Countless tastings in their cellar with its four guardsmen ranks of huge oak barrels convinced me that their reputation was thoroughly deserved. Both of them taught me a lot about the technicalities of wine but it was Marcel, talking of his vintages with a religious tenderness, who taught me something about the poetry of wine.

Astonishingly, I also met Claude in the bistro—astonishingly because, as far as anyone could tell, he worked a twenty-four-hour day with a consequent lack of time for social outings. Claude was the local printer, constantly bedevilled by wine-growers wanting 20,000 labels by five o'clock the same afternoon. He managed nonetheless to be unvaryingly good-tempered and even readier than my other benign friends to render a service. One way and another, I must have pestered Claude rather more often than Paul or Maxime.

Although we never got on first-name terms, I had a particular liking for the *garde champêtre*, a combination of district gamekeeper and messenger boy for the mayor's office in our village. He had no powers of arrest but on encountering some major misdeanour—allowing a dog to wander unleashed through the vineyards, for example—he could deliver a summons. His uniform consisted of whatever he chose to put on but he was never seen without his regulation *képi* and when carrying out his official duties he assumed an austere, almost a forbidding expression, and stamped martially rather than walked. Seeing him in this persona it was hard to believe that he could possibly have his lighter moments.

I discovered that he did one day when we bumped into each other in the beautiful old hill town which overlooked our valley. That we should meet so far from home—a good seven or eight kilometres—was an event. The *garde* greeted me, I thought, with relief. Thrust among an alien population, he was enchanted to see a familiar face.

'Monsieur Karshev! What brings you to the metropolis?'

'Just wandering around, *Monsieur le Garde*.'

'Me, I came to deliver a paper—an official document, you

understand. So here you are and here am I. You know what I think? I think it calls for a glass of wine. What do you say?'

'What do I say, *Monsieur le Garde*? Why, I say that it's indispensable.'

To this day I haven't any idea why the *garde champêtre* should have found my reply so irresistibly comic. I looked on with some perturbation as he doubled up, gyrated wildly, waved his arms about in uncontrollable delight and emitted not so much a series of guffaws as a single indefinitely sustained bellow. It was some time before he could speak. When he had recovered, '*Eh, oui,*' he said between renewed spasms, '*vous l'avez bien dit—eh, oui, c'est indispensable*! Indispensable— that's the word all right!' While we were drinking our wine in the nearest café, the *garde* was twice compelled to put his glass down in order to erupt in a further paroxysm. '*Ah, ça alors, c'est le cas de le dire—c'est indispensable*!'

Official business seemed to oblige the *garde* to spend much of his time in Monsieur Boin's café. Whenever I dropped in myself for an aperitif, he would leer at me as though we had both passed the previous night in some outrageous orgy. Then, the leer expanding into a joyous smile, he would nudge me slyly in the ribs. '*Alors, Monsieur Karshev—c'est indispensable, hein?*' and he would go off into a prolonged fit of hilarity. I'd be surprised if Oscar Wilde's quips were ever received with such wholehearted enthusiasm. Whoever else might find me rather dull company, the *garde* regarded me, never ceased to regard me, as the greatest wag he had ever come across. If I'd owned a dog, I dare say I could have let it romp freely in the vineyards all day long and the *garde* would have done no more than nudge me and whisper as between accomplices, '*Eh, bien, Monsieur Karkhov—c'est indispensable, non?*'

CHAPTER TEN

The *garde's* authority was not restricted to errant dogs. He was required to eject whatever other animals he might encounter among the vines (years before he had had to expel a wild boar which had come lumbering in from the nearby forest and this was a saga which he could be persuaded to narrate without having to be pushed). He was likewise empowered should he catch anyone shooting in the vineyards when the grapes were ripening to send the offender before the magistrates. He was, in short, the accredited protector of the vineyards, their tutelary deity. His other activities were looked on as secondary by everyone except himself. Adjusting his *képi*, '*Non, Monsieur,*' he would say sternly when urged to devote himself exclusively to the defence of the vines, '*non, Monsieur*, I am a servant of the State and must observe *all* the obligations incumbent on a man in my position.' My neighbours couldn't see it. They would have liked a watchtower to be installed in every vineyard and a dozen *gardes* to patrol around the clock. The vineyards were sacred.

'Do you happen to know,' I asked my friend, Roger, 'when wine was first grown in the district?'

'*Eh, bien*, let me see. As far as I know, the first winegrower in our family was my great-great-grandfather. Before him it was the Romans.'

Roger had the peasant's inborn sense of continuity. To his way of thinking the Romans had only just got in ahead of his great-great-grandfather. He sounded slightly peeved that a bunch of foreigners should have sneaked in and laid a prior claim.

I didn't know enough to dispute this snippet of history. For all I could say to the contrary, the Romans might well have been the first to introduce grapes into the region. Equally, it was quite on the cards, as the locals liked to maintain, that our hill town was actually founded by Julius Caesar himself. There had certainly been a Roman encampment on the site. Coins with the heads of some of Julius's less illustrious successors were still unearthed in the fields.

'What do you suppose the Romans thought of the wine around here?'

'*Mon vieux*, it's well known—they loved it, they couldn't get enough of it. Do you wonder? When you think of the sort of muck the poor devils had to drink at home.'

Here again, I didn't venture to ask Roger how he could be so confident about what the Romans thought of the local wine and how they evaluated it in relation to their own product. I thought it would be more tactful, too, to avoid hinting that a testimonial bequeathed by the Romans would not be worth much anyway. The chances were that their taste in wine was as defective as their taste in everything else. When it came to oenology, I was prepared to back curés against Romans any day. Curés had always been known and respected as discriminating drinkers. The most intransigent atheists, agnostics, freethinkers and anticlericals were only too happy to tamp down their prejudices in order to get some tips on wine from any curé who felt disposed to give them.

Modern curés can't be counted on to anything like the same extent. They tend to be hearty up-to-date fellows who wear sports shirts, take a keen interest in ecology and vote socialist. What they drink I couldn't say. My guess would be that they stick to mineral water so as to keep in shape for next week's Rugby match.

The curé in whose parish I was living had nothing in common with the brisk go-ahead types who came after him. He was one of the old school which was always my favourite school in respect of curés and anybody or anything else. You wouldn't have caught him drinking mineral water. He drank wine with humility and spoke of it with veneration. He spoke with less veneration of the soutane which he wore winter and summer alike. About this he grumbled incessantly.

'Of all the damnable impractical garments ever invented! In wet weather it gets waterlogged and trails in the mud, in dry weather it's stifling and collects the dust. Thank Heavens, at least I don't have to sleep in it. Clergymen, I'm told, can wear anything they choose. Lucky clergymen! Perhaps I'd better convert to Protestantism' and he would laugh gustily.

A glass of wine could always restore his good humour. After visiting his parishioners he would often call on me for a chat. The neighbours had their own wine and nothing else. I had some bottles of white Burgundy, some Alsace and when, as didn't often happen, I was flush, a bottle or two of champagne. I think the curé was glad of an opportunity to drink something other than the local vintages but also I think he really enjoyed my company. I certainly enjoyed his. Like all good Frenchmen he was respectful of writers or artists of any kind.

'Now I wonder, *cher Monsieur*, whether I might ask a great favour?'

'Of course, *mon Père*, what can I do for you?'

'Why, I'd be very pleased if perhaps you could let me have a copy of one of your books.'

I gave him a little volume of poems which had been published a short while before. He appeared to be gratified. I was gratified by his gratification.

'How I regret that I don't know English! And I must make a confession to you. One of my many defects is that I cannot read poetry.'

'There are plenty of people, *mon Père*, who'll tell you that I can't write it.'

I had almost as much success with this little quip as I'd had when I introduced the *garde* to '*indispensable.*'

When he visited me next, he brought me a present in return, a rough Celtic cross in what I took to be a strange light-coloured stone. I was surprised. It was not in character for the curé to press symbols of his faith on unbelievers like myself.

'No, no, *cher Monsieur*! I'm not hoping to convert you, be reassured! The object is of a purely temporal interest.'

'Which is what, *mon Père*?'

119

'Why, I'm sure you know about the phylloxera which wiped out all the vines of France towards the end of last century? Well, our winegrowers made these little crosses out of camphor which they fancied would eradicate the insects. So what you have there is not stone as you may have thought but petrified camphor. Fifty years ago the peasants quite often dug up these crosses. They're very rarely found now and are practically never found intact.'

'And they were made in the shape of a cross, I take it, so as to exorcise the demon responsible for the phylloxera?'

'I'm afraid not, *cher Monsieur*. The shape was simply so that the thing could be lodged more firmly at the root of the vine.'

In the eighteenth century, one of our curé's predecessors was the Abbé Poupard who wrote a history of the district. The wines produced in the parish seem to have had him dancing in the vestry. He forthrightly pronounced them sound, delicious, refreshing, excellent, admirable, exquisite and a great many other praiseworthy things besides. No doubt they were; but no one could have foreseen that one day gourmets would be appreciatively sniffing at them as though they were Montrachets, masticating them as a preliminary to swallowing them, and earnestly rating them in terms of their acidity, their fruitiness, their aftertaste and their excess or lack of ethyl alcohol. Still less could it have been anticipated that these gourmets would be licking their lips in America, in England, in Scandinavia, in Japan and—a staggering thought—in the *terra incognita*, in Australia.

Laboratory analyses, test tubes, controlled temperatures and subtle adjustments to improve quality in a poor year were refinements which had never been heard of when I first turned up. Maxime, Paul, Roger and the others made their wine very nearly as their fathers, grandfathers, great-great-grandfathers— and conceivably the Romans—had done. Grapes for the production of white wine went into the press and the juice was transferred to oak casks and left to get on with it. Red wine necessitated a rather more complicated procedure.

Unpressed, the grapes were heaped into a great wooden tank. As they fermented a crust formed on the surface. This had to be pushed back into the mash.

The pushing was something not to be missed. Removing his boots, his socks (if he wore such effeminate fripperies) and his trousers, the *vigneron* or his chosen representative would bound into the tank, grab hold of a wooden crossbar and trample away until the crust was reabsorbed. Once in a while the trampler would bend his head too far down and get a whiff of the carbonic gas which rose invisibly from the bubbling mixture. Should he have been mad enough to start his trampling when he was alone in the cellar, he would be unconscious within seconds and, unless rescued, would most likely drown. It did sometimes happen. 'A great way to go,' was the customary obituary. 'Drowning in wine—ah, let's hope we all have such a wonderful death!'

A high-spirited young woman who was staying with us became even more high-spirited while watching the treading of the grapes. Further stimulated by several glasses of the previous year's vintage, she shed shoes, stockings and skirt, clambered into the tank and trampled exuberantly. Nothing remotely resembling this spectacle had ever been seen before. The women of the hamlet—women everywhere in the rural districts—were on the prim side. In no circumstances could they have been induced to remove their stockings, let alone their skirts, in the presence of a group of males—probably not in the presence of their own husbands. There was a moment, a long moment, of stupefaction, followed by a positive cloudburst of applause. At one bound—you might say at one trample—the young woman became the heroine of a rustic saga. The *garde*'s wild boar was nothing in comparison. Ever afterwards, not two members of her audience could meet without recalling the incident. Those who had not been among the spectators were given accounts of it which became increasingly piquant.

'Well, you should have been there, *mon vieux*, that's all I can say, you should have been there! You've never seen anything like it, never. Off came the skirt—*eh, oui, mon vieux*—and that was only the beginning. Next the blouse and, believe it or not, then the brassière. Not a stitch on, naked as an earthworm, *et hop*! Into the tank! *Et une sacrée belle fille*! *Avec une jolie paire de nichons*! Ah, you missed a treat!'

The treading of grapes implied a healthy disregard for microbes. After the hysterical fears which prevailed in Paris and every other city this came as a relief. Le Biguin (he may have had a more conventional name but nobody ever used it) was pre-eminent in his disdain for hygienic precautions. He was the innocent of the hamlet, not like me a mere figurative simpleton, a genuine idiot, but I admired his commonsense. He was also afflicted with a cleft palate. Neither disability altered the fact that he had inherited some exceptional vines from a distant relative and made the best wine in the immediate vicinity.

Le Biguin rather took to me and I never passed his tumbledown shed (he had no cellar properly speaking) without him hailing me. The combination of his cleft palate and his Berrichon *patois* rather hindered conversation but that was of no importance. He spoke rarely, anyway. As far as I could tell, he simply liked to pass the time of day with me, instinctively drawn to a fellow imbecile, I suppose. I reciprocated his affection, no doubt for the same reason.

A hatch outside Le Biguin's shed served some obscure purpose. With an American visitor (it was George, my credulous friend from the rue de Charonne) I passed by one day when it was blocked up and filled with an overflow of wine. Le Biguin was trying to unblock it. His hairy forearms were thrust into the wine up to the elbow. He called out something incomprehensible to us. The fact that I couldn't understand him didn't matter. I knew what he was proposing. 'Yes, thanks, Biguin, I'd love one.'

The glass he produced was so thickly encased in grime as to be completely opaque. Le Biguin wiped it on his greasy trousers without making any perceptible difference in its appearance and dipped it into the hatch. Forearms or no forearms the wine tasted as good as ever. Beside me, George was shuddering. Le Biguin filled the same glass from the same source and handed it to George.

Raised in the American tradition of antiseptics, sanitation and bacteriophobia, George received it as though it was a scorpion. His expression was one of insupportable revulsion weirdly combined with a grateful smile for Le Biguin's benefit.

Out of the corner of his mouth, 'Alister, for Christ's sake do something. I can't drink this, I *can't*.'

'You've got to, George. Le Biguin will be terribly offended if you don't.'

'Oh, Jesus . . . !'

George had been a pilot in the US Air Force during the war and his courage in action, so I'd been assured, was notorious. None of his wartime exploits can have demanded anything like the same degree of bravery with which, his face the colour of seaweed and his throat muscles jumping erratically up and down, he finally swallowed Le Biguin's wine. He told me subsequently that he had expected, at the very least, to suffer a bad bout of typhoid.

If he had, Le Biguin would not have displayed any noticeable concern. From November of one year to September of the next he was never seen to look happy or unhappy or angry or worried or excited or disgruntled or anything else. Only in October did his features express some emotion although it was impossible to say what. October was the month of the grape harvest, the *vendange*, and Le Biguin was not alone in getting a bit on edge as it drew near.

Much depended on what sort of mood St Vincent was in. St Vincent was the patron saint of winegrowers. That was another of the mysteries, like the origin of Tayaux. Why was St Vincent selected for this vital role? I never heard that he was a Friar Tuck, a wine-swigging bon vivant. When I looked him up in the encyclopaedia I learnt that he was the reverse, a very austere churchman indeed. I also learnt that he was a Spaniard. I'd heard from my neighbours what they thought of Spanish wine and I decided against telling them their saint's nationality. It might have caused a schism. My friend the curé came up with an explanation as to why St Vincent should have become the winegrowers' patron. It could, he thought, have been for no other reason that that his name began with the noble syllable '*vin*'.

What preoccupied the whole district as the grapes approached maturity was whether St Vincent would see to it that no hailstorms occurred. Floods, typhoons, landslides could be handled; but not *cette saloperie de grêle* which tore the grapes to pieces and, when violent enough, could so damage the branches of the vines as to harm the harvest not only for that year but equally for the year following.

Defensive measures had been foreseen in case St Vincent fell down on the job. The instant hail seemed to be imminent, the grower on hail duty for the day would rush off to a small hut in one of the outlying fields. This was a mini-arsenal, crammed with enough rockets to wage a fair-sized war. They were fired into the threatening clouds. Sometimes after the barrage it hailed anyway, sometimes not. Either way, confidence in the efficacy of the rockets was undiminished. Next time the sky looked as if it might be up to mischief, off went the rockets again.

Hail or no hail, the grapes had to be picked. The vineyards were tiny then, amounting to no more than two or three acres each. A single grower might have half-a-dozen such patches. They would be widely scattered over the hillsides but he and his family (except for the grandmothers, fully occupied with their goats) could do all the picking without extra help. Neighbours who hadn't yet started their own harvesting or who had already finished might offer their assistance but it wasn't really needed, it was merely an excuse for being together.

Later on, when the local wine had begun to acquire a reputation, outside pickers had to be hired—some of them from as far away as the Nivernais on the other side of the Loire. Overnight the population of the hamlet increased by two hundred per cent. This incursion was the only change that ever took place in the district of which I was all in favour. We all were. There was no denying that the pickers were foreigners as defined by our standards but they wouldn't be around for long and meantime they created an unaccustomed animation which was as exciting as a circus.

Varied provisions were made for their accommodation—a bed of straw in the loft, a sleeping-bag in the stables, a tent rigged up from horse-blankets or, if nothing else could be arranged, a pile of hessian bags on the ground. They earned their wages. Crouching down all day to snip off the bunches of grapes and then lugging them in great wickerwork baskets to the cart which would transport them to the cellar was backbreaking work. Moreover, St Vincent, for some inscrutable reason, never came up with the right sort of weather for the *vendange*. It was always too hot or too wet. The pickers suffered very nearly as much as the curé in his soutane.

They should, of course, have gone whining to some official busybody that they were being exploited. Apparently it never occurred to them. I could see why. The work may have been hard and the accommodation rudimentary but the pay wasn't too bad and the side benefits were considerable. At the end of the day when everyone congregated in the cellar they were free to help themselves to as much wine as they wanted. By the time dinner was served in the communal kitchen, the most insistent trade unionist wouldn't have got a whimper out of them.

Those dinners were appalling in their abundance. I would have been satiated after finishing the hors d'oeuvres. I was close to being satiated merely by looking at them. The pickers never left a scrap on their plates. Cornets of ham filled with mayonnaise, artichokes, olives, tomatoes, pâtés, bulging country loaves—down went the whole lot. Then they were ready for the meat, the vegetables, the cheese, the salad and the pudding. With the coffee they drank the ferocious *marc* of the region.

Instead of being comatose after these orgies, they were stimulated to song. Normally I was the only inhabitant of the hamlet who was not in bed by nine o'clock. When the grape-pickers were around it would be midnight before the glee club ended its performance. The accordions were ill played and the choruses off-key but we wouldn't have swapped those concerts for a recital by La Callas.

Those were the good old days. Everyone thought they were good—the *vignerons*, the pickers and, when I sidled into one of the cellars to drink a glass or two with the rest of the company at nightfall, me. St Vincent, too, very likely. But the good old days were, as always, too good to last. With the expansion of the vineyards, it wasn't possible to get enough pickers even by going further than the Nivernais, to such distant lands as Vendée or Brittany or to Paris itself, the city of dreadful night. Italians and Portuguese and Spaniards had to be called on. They arrived as a rule in their own cars, sometimes with caravans attached. They waived their right to those prodigious meals which used to be provided by the grower and his wife, preferring to drive off in their cars to dine at a nearby bistro. It wouldn't have been so bad if they had entertained us in the evenings with an occasional Neapolitan folk song, a Portuguese *saudade* or a Spanish *cante jondo*. No such luck. I never even heard a performance of 'Waltzing Matilda' although Australians were among the pickers during at least two of these latter-day harvests. The only songs to be heard came from the transistor radios with which everyone seemed to be equipped.

The wine tasted just as good, though.

CHAPTER ELEVEN

The *vendange*, when it was still what a *vendange* ought to be, was unquestionably the liveliest time of the year but it was not our only distraction even if the range of entertainments was limited. The nearest cinema was in a town twenty kilometres away. It showed antiquated films once a week, frequently with ill-timed interruptions when the projector broke down and always in conditions of extreme discomfort. Since there wasn't a single car in the hamlet anyway, it would have been difficult to get to this amusement, supposing anyone had wanted to or could afford to. As in all wine-growing districts, there were some agreeable restaurants not far away. However, these were no more affordable than the cinema. Perhaps twice each year, a forlorn touring circus would set up its tents but, again, at a site not easily reached.

Lack of money likewise ruled out any possibility of holidays. Most of my neighbours had never left the district except when they were shunted off somewhere or other at the age of eighteen to do their military service. Thereafter it was out of the question to absent themselves. Grandmothers were capable of looking after goats but it would have been madness to entrust them with pigs and cows, and nobody could afford to hire farmhands. The suffering urban proletariat went off every year to the hills or the seaside on their five weeks' paid leave. Leave for the peasants consisted of a brief spell on Saturday afternoon chez *Monsieur Boin* or *La Rose*.

But lack of money and lack of standardised entertainments couldn't diminish their natural gaiety. In Paris, where the same *joie de vivre* had so captivated me in the early days, poverty was progressively disappearing. So was the *joie de vivre*. It was slowly—and not so very slowly—being smothered by the alien society which the ministers of newness and their colleagues were instituting. The intellectuals, influential in Paris as nowhere else, were indefatigable when it came to purveying the gospel of moroseness. A tiny beleaguered group of people like Pierre and Alain went on resisting but it was only a matter of time, it sometimes seemed, before laughter was forbidden by edict. There were a few curmudgeons in the country, too, but most of the peasants I knew had a capacity for enjoyment which didn't need the stimulus of films or restaurants or anything else.

With no television to daze them, they would spend their short evenings—it was unheard of to go to bed later than ten o'clock—talking together in one or another kitchen in front of the wood-burning stove which served for heating as well as cooking and which, in winter and summer alike, was never allowed to go out. When I was lucky enough to be present, I was always struck by the acuity and independence of their comments. I could guess why this should be so. The Paris intellectuals I'd encountered—like the intellectuals everywhere else—took their opinions from whatever partisan newspaper or review they happened to be addicted to. The peasants never read anything, some of them couldn't have done so if they'd wanted to. Apart from my eccentric self, I don't suppose anyone in the hamlet ever owned a book. I never saw one. If there were any, they must have been hidden away in the loft along with other curios accumulated by chance over the years. The peasants' opinions were their own, not something which they'd been bamboozled into believing by some self-assured theorist with the gift of the gab.

It's not quite true that no one ever read anything. We had the local newspaper. That kept us abreast of what was going on in the world—our world. It came out weekly and I always admired its sense of proportion. Other newspapers gave over the front page to the outbreak of war or revolution. The lead story in our paper would be more likely to deal with the outbreak of mildew. In one issue I saw, the whole of page one was taken up with a gripping survey of the region's cheeses and the whole of page two with the first instalment of a series on artificial fertilisers which had me fretting throughout the intervening week while waiting to see how the sequel would turn out.

Of course, I never had the necessary technical background to get the full benefit of the cheese and fertiliser items. I tended to concentrate more on the social notes. These were detailed enough to keep us occupied for days. I remember an account of the wedding of a corn chandler's daughter from a village across the hill which filled three columns. It was like reading a chapter from Balzac.

The really important event of the week, however, was the tour of the hamlet every Saturday evening. It was an informal affair but as obligatory as feeding the pigs or pruning the vines. Unannounced, Maxime, say, would drop in on me. A glass of wine and we would go off together to see, as it might be, Paul. After another glass, the three of us would pay a visit to Roger, then all four would call on Philippe, and so on. No gargantuan tumblers were brought out during these excursions. We drank no more than one glass at each cellar, a glass of moderate size. The 'tour' had nothing in common with an Australian or English pub crawl. We weren't out to get befuddled. The aim was simply to be together and we drank as a token of our fellowship.

My participation in these gatherings gave me the sort of satisfaction that other varieties of snob get out of frequenting the rich or the titled or the celebrated. It was a rare privilege for a foreigner and one who was not a peasant to be admitted to this society; and I was conscious of it. I couldn't join in the discussions of arcane subjects like mildew and the relative merits of chalky and flinty soils; but after I had picked up some fragments of the *patois* and had become accustomed to the Berrichon accent, I listened with fascination to the stories that were told of bygone calamities, disputes, comic mishaps, memorable revellings, notable vintages and notable personalities.

I was destined to figure as a notable personality myself in one of these narratives. Coming back from the village one winter evening, I decided to take a short cut over the hill among the vines. It was already dark, I mistook the path and wandered around for ten minutes before getting on the right track. When I reached the hamlet, I bumped into Maxime and mentioned casually that I'd lost my way.

'Lost your way! *Non, mais c'est pas vrai*! Between the village and here you lost your way? Two kilometres in a straight line and you lost your way! How could you lose your way?'

'I don't *know* how I lost my way. I just did. It may sound silly but there it is. I lost my way. So how about we drop the subject?'

'You lost your way! *C'est pas possible*!'

I could see from Maxime's expression what was happening. He was thinking what a story this would make and the pleasure he would have in recounting it. Another saga was in the making, it would enter the repertoire along with the story of Françoise's baptism or the young woman trampling the grapes. I didn't object to being the hero of a saga. It made me feel like Beowulf or Havelok the Dane.

I heard the saga recited, with abundant embellishments, more than once because the mere fact that I was present didn't inhibit Maxime or the attendant chorus in the least.

'*Eh, bien, mon vieux*, this Alistairre of ours lost his way! Remember his yarns about Australia—hundreds of kilometres without a horse or a road to be seen? Well, it's *two* kilometres from the village to here and he lost his way! You're not going to believe it but he told me himself he'd tried to navigate by the stars and of course he got more confused than ever. A miserable city-dweller trying to navigate by the stars! *Ah, mon pauvre Alistairre*, perhaps you'd better take a compass with you next time you go out of doors.'

'So that's who it was! I might have guessed. I heard someone yelling his head off. *Non, mais dis donc, Alistairre*, aren't you ashamed of yourself getting into such a panic? Two kilometres!'

'A panic is right. It'll be a long time before I forget the sight of you when you got back! Shaking in every limb!'

'*N'y a pas à dire*, you're the only man who could lose himself two kilometres away.'

I had become a part of local history . . .

There was a genuinely historic event at which I was present, although only as an onlooker. I was talking with Maxime and his wife one evening in their kitchen. A friend of theirs arrived unexpectedly. He was carrying a *vielle*, that ancient stringed instrument with a crankhandle and a small keyboard. A tricky thing to play but when the performer is good the music of the *vielle* is as irresistible to a Berrichon as an accordion to a Parisian.

The friend was a virtuoso. He began to play a traditional *bourrée*. No Berrichon could resist that antique dance, either. Without a word said, Maxime and Suzanne began to go through the movements. Sylvain, three years old, was playing outside. The music, the stamping feet and my applause brought him in. '*Viens, mon p'tit Sylvain*,' said Maxime and under his guidance Sylvain became, surely, the only Australian ever to dance a *bourrée*.

Between us, we attracted others besides Sylvain. Roger came in and, without pausing to greet the rest of us, immediately began dancing. Le Biguin, ordinarily so timid that he averted his eyes when he encountered anyone except me, his brother simpleton, came stumbling in from his shack next door. His mother, Isabelle, bent and creaking, was with him. She must have been well over eighty but, with everyone applauding, she joined in energetically and expertly. Within ten minutes the whole population of the hamlet was dancing the *bourrée* in Suzanne's kitchen. We were transported a hundred years back.

To hear the *vielle* played and see the *bourrée* danced today you would have to go to a self-conscious 'folklore' festival. I was perhaps the last person who will ever see a group of French peasants spontaneously engaged in the same pastime as their forebears centuries ago.

More ceremonious festivities also took place, and still take place, from time to time. Baptisms, first communions and fortieth, but only fortieth, birthdays were the occasion for feasts which made the meals provided for the grape-pickers look like Salvation Army handouts. At one of them, I was seated next to the *garde*. Both of us were in the habit of boasting that we could drink the other under the table. '*Allons, Monsieur Alistairre*,' the *garde* kept urging me during this particular contest, 'drink up! Ah, you Australians are a poor lot! This is how we do it in the Berry!' and down went another pint of sturdy red wine. To get a breathing space, I turned to my neighbour on the other side. When I turned back—no *garde*. A search was at once organised. The *garde* was discovered where he had always claimed no amount of wine could put him— under the table.

But it was weddings which headed the list of our amuse- ments. Until I came to live in the country my experience of weddings had been limited to the Parisian variety. Cheerless affairs they were. True, the mayor officiating at the civil ceremony would do his best. He would wear his tricolour sash of office with a jaunty air, he would beam like the Cheeryble Brothers and he would deliver a little homily about how happy the Republic was to see two young people hand in hand starting out in life. But his efforts weren't really enough to make things go with a swing.

It wasn't the Parisians' fault that their marriages were so lacklustre. They were confronted with too many constraints. The traffic, to begin with. In the country, a parade down the village street with a *vielliste* at the head, was mandatory. It would have been a troublesome business identifying the remains if a bridal procession had trailed down the middle of the rue de la Paix or the Boulevard St Germain.

Then there were the clothes that were sometimes worn at our rural weddings. When Maxime's son got married, for instance, nearly everyone was wearing the costume of the region—long woven skirts, embroidered blouses and lace headgear for the women, corduroy trousers, white gaiters, fancy waistcoats and beribboned hats for the men. They made a wonderfully picturesque spectacle but in Paris they would have provoked unfavourable reactions. In the sixteenth *arrondisse-*

ment passers-by would have looked away with genteel embarrassment, in the Latin Quarter the louts in their squalid leather jackets and carefully ripped jeans would have jeered maliciously.

Nor could Parisians hope to get away with the fusillades which are inseparable from a Berrichon marriage. All our weddings are, you might say, shotgun weddings. Traditionally, on the night preceding the event, the young men of the district wander in a body through the vineyards blasting away at nothing. No one had thought it worthwhile to warn me that marriages in the Berry were announced not with a peal of bells, as elsewhere, but with a peal of ordnance. A peasant uprising was the only explanation I could imagine the first time I heard a fearsome rattle of musketry at midnight. I wasn't too alarmed, though. The uprising might have been directed at the taxation authorities or some similar irksome body, hardly at me. If I'd been the target, guns wouldn't have been necessary. It would have been enough to instruct the fourteen-year-old Jean-Marc to clobber me. In the same circumstances, Parisians would have concluded that civil war had broken out and would have been quaking down in the cellar within five minutes.

The cannonade doesn't stop with the dawn of the wedding day. During the ceremony, all the lads who have been letting fly throughout the night take up their station to the side of the church door. As bride and groom emerge, a thunderous salvo is fired. Heads of State, I reflected more than once, think a lot of themselves because they rate a 21-gun salute. Twenty-one shots would be dismissed as a very stingy tribute in the Berry. I'd put the number fired for a Berrichon marriage at several hundred.

I'd be surprised, too, if any Head of State was ever so liberally treated in the matter of food and drink as we were when weddings were celebrated, when Raymonde and Pascal married their daughter, for example. Not that we were the only ones to benefit from their notion of hospitality. Barrels of wine had been set up in the village square and any passer-by was welcome to help himself. But the whole of that wedding was on a heroic scale. Luncheon, I suppose, lasted from one o'clock to five. We were then liberated so that we could digest before going on the next stage—pre-dinner drinks and an inexhaustible buffet. By eight o'clock, everyone except me was feeling peckish again and ready to hoe into a dinner which lasted until midnight. Then, always with the same exception, everyone danced until dawn when some garlic sausage and red wine was consumed: it kept them going until lunchtime when the substantial leftovers from the buffet were gobbled up. What went on thereafter I couldn't say. Something, undoubtedly; but I had cravenly retreated long before, amiably derided by the company for my lack of stamina.

I'm not sure that the Berrichons themselves always have enough stamina to confront without quailing, a little ceremony conducted on the morning following a marriage. With much guffawing, a select group arrives at the home of the newlyweds carrying the classic post-wedding gift—a chamber pot filled with tawny champagne and lumps of melted chocolate, the whole bearing a nauseating resemblance to the normal contents of a chamber pot. Awakened by the visitors' merry laughter, the groom is not merely expected to show his appreciation of this bucolic humour but to take a hearty swig of the loathsome compound. I'd like to see a Parisian try to get that down.

Then there is an additional and, as far as I know, inexplicable ritual to be performed when either the bride or groom is the last child of his or her family to be married. In such cases, all the inhabitants of the hamlet concerned are required to put out one or two broomsticks on the night following the marriage. At some point in the dead vast and middle of the night, the couple's friends go from house to house to collect them. They'd better be there, too. Failure to comply with the custom means that the guilty householder may legitimately be aroused and fined two brooms or, should he be an habitual offender, three.

Transported to a convenient field, the sticks are piled up and set alight. A hat belonging to the groom's father and an item of underwear belonging to the bride's mother are added to the bonfire and, in obedience to some strange pagan mystery, everyone takes it in turn to jump over the flames. Only then is the couple regarded as lawfully married.

When no weddings are due to be celebrated, one can always hope for a funeral to provide some fun. The men of the district have never been ostentatiously pious. They see to it that the curé is sent for urgently if they suspect that they might be on their deathbeds and that is about as far as it goes. They rarely attend Mass. They leave it to their womenfolk to put in a good word for them each Sunday. Funerals, however, unfailingly bring the entire male population to the church. A funeral is virtually the only recognised justification for taking a morning off.

A suitable appearance of melancholy is maintained while the Mass is underway. At its conclusion, the women linger outside the church and collaborate in recounting every detail of the drama, beginning with the onset of whatever disease carried the victim off and proceeding to the administration of the last rites and the ultimate death rattle. The men visibly relax and head for the café. There might be some perfunctory allusions to the deceased but these don't go on for long. Someone will remark that his wine had always been palatable, someone else will hint that it was sometimes a bit too tannic and that will be that. Sitting around in a café—and on a working day! It's a rare dissipation and one to be savoured. One could be grateful to the corpse for having provided the opportunity but it would be idiotic to spoil things by sanctimonious groaning over his departure.

Offhand, I can only think of one other day in the year when you can be confident of seeing all the men of the hamlet in their pews—the Feast of St Vincent. Understandably, they take the view that it would be crazy to risk affronting their saint. But attendance at church, while a reasonable precaution, is a relatively minor part of the day's carryings-on. St Vincent is primarily honoured—as, of course, he should be—by the pouring of wine.

The winegrowers take it in turn to serve as *batonnier*, whose badge of office is a *baton* or wooden staff surmounted by an effigy of the saint. Bearing this aloft, the *batonnier* leads the assembly from the church to the village hall where he has installed a barrel of white and a barrel of red wine. There is also a table on which are laid out a number of *galettes*. You're bound to eat some. Failure to do so would be deemed not only an insult to the *batonnier* but to St Vincent himself. Personally, I always considered that it was the *galette* which was insulting, insulting to any normal palate, that is.

According to the dictionary, a *galette* is 'a flat cake made out of puff pastry'. The dictionary has got it wrong. It's flat certainly; I've never choked down anything flatter. That it's made from puff pastry or any other edible substance cannot be true. All the *galettes* I've ever eaten suggested that the ingredients consisted of stagnant water and the sweepings from Monsieur Vattan's carpentry workship. The consistency is such that your jaws are cemented together after one bite. If you happen to have a rabid dog to muzzle, a *galette* is just what you need.

My personal calendar was made up of such moments—gnawing my way through a *galette* at some festivity or other, losing my way and thereby becoming part of an imperishable folklore, attending weddings and funerals, joining impromptu gatherings in a neighbour's cellar. Days (except for the Feast of St Vincent) and weeks and months didn't come into it. For a year or two I was aware of the seasons. In Australia, or so I seemed to remember, we moved from summer to winter without any intervening cycle. In the Berry, I saw for the first time what autumn was, the vines stripped of their leaves and looking like black driftwood that could not possibly ever come to life again. The first minute glitter of green on the bare trees, infinitessimal to the point that one had to look closely to be quite sure that it was really there, was a recurring astonishment at the beginning of each spring.

Then the seasons, too, began to blur. My friends were very much aware of them. They had to be. The seasons dictated their work, their lives. But, after a while, a long while, summer, autumn, winter, spring, although they were as marvellous as ever in their sharply defined variety, ceased to be timekeepers for me. As in Paris, I gradually gave up counting the months and years. As in Paris, if someone had asked me for how long I'd been living in the hamlet, I would have said, 'Oh, two or three years.' But it wasn't, I abruptly realised, two or three years or four or five but a great deal longer. My friends were growing older, some of them—Isabelle, Le Biguin—had died. The boys I had known as children had, impossibly, become old enough to take over from their fathers, my own children were no longer children. I was growing older myself, much older. Even if I hadn't in my timeless state noticed it while it was happening, there had been other changes, a lot of them. And I suddenly became conscious of these, too.

CHAPTER TWELVE

Try as I might, I hadn't been able to feel that any of the changes in Paris were for the better. I was never able to delight in the glass pyramid or the Cultural Centre, drugstores and pubs seemed a dismal substitute for cafés, and I got no satisfaction from the express motorway along the banks of the Seine. The changes which overtook my part of the Berry didn't have me snarling to anything like the same extent. The minister of newness was busy elsewhere.

Not that all the changes had me cheering. I never quite resigned myself, for instance, to the loss of witches. They had virtually disappeared before I got here and this saddened me. I'd been looking forward to them. Historically, the Berry outranked all the provinces of France when it came to flying around on broomsticks and casting disagreeable spells. During the great sorcery trials of the seventeenth century, you could be pretty confident that a handful of Berrichons or Berrichonnes would be among the accused and every variety of wizard and warlock went on getting up to mischief for a long time afterwards. By the 1930s they were on the way out but I didn't know this and I expected to be bumping into them within a week of my arrival.

I thought I'd been lucky enough to find a witch right on my doorstep in the person of the aged Isabelle. She had the looks for it—long straggly hair, a slight beard, two lonely fangs in her jaws, a hooked nose. It was a disappointment when she turned out to be the kindliest old creature in the world who was forever bestowing apples on my children. She had the reputation of being an admirable cook but given an eye of newt and a wing of bat I doubt if she would have known how to prepare them.

A couple of centuries ago, three of the nearby villages were

especially notorious for the prevalence of necromantic abom-
inations. One of them still pays tribute to its illustrious past
by organising a 'Feast of the Sorcerers' each year when
participants wear white sheets and death's-head masks. It
shows the right spirit but the revellers only drink wine, not
cat's blood, human sacrifices play no part in the ceremonies
and nothing that could fairly be described as an orgy terminates
the proceedings.

Black Masses, by all accounts, used to be celebrated in every
convenient forest clearing and I was really rather moved when
someone told me that on these occasions the Devil showed a
delicate tact with which he is not ordinarily credited. Elsewhere, he has always chosen to appear before his devotees in
the shape of a goat. But goats, producers of the succulent local
cheeses, are highly respected animals in the Berry. Purely out
of consideration for this pro-goat sentiment, the Devil appears
in the Berry, and only in the Berry, as a horse.

But he appears less and less frequently. I've never met anyone who has seen him. I do have some friends who are
acquainted with a witch or two and they were good enough
to introduce me to one. She was a disappointment. She might
have been a retired schoolmistress. Isabelle looked infinitely
more witch-like. I said '*Bonjour, Madame*' and she said
'*Bonjour, Monsieur*'. Then she asked me how long I'd lived
in France and I told her. She surmised that the *vendange*
promised to be a good one and I agreed. Then we said goodbye.
It wasn't my idea of what a conversation with a witch ought
to be. There was no evidence that she'd ever cast a spell on
a neighbour's cow, let alone caused the cow's owner to go down
with typhoid or gout. I could more easily imagine her calling
on a suffering neighbour with patent medicines and bowls of
nourishing soup.

At least I didn't have to witness the dissolution of the covens.
The *patois*, on the other hand, with its marvellously esoteric
vocabulary, its unaccountable elisions and its odd structures,
expired beneath my very eyes. I'm not likely to be called on
again to serve as interpreter between a Berrichon and a

Marseillais. You'll hear it spoken in an attenuated form by older people between themselves but mostly they speak the same French as in Lyons or Paris or Nantes. The younger generation has forgotten all but an occasional word or phrase. Television has arrived.

There's some consolation to be found for the decline of witchcraft and the erosion of the *patois* in the improvement of the wine. It was pretty much of a lucky dip when first I came here. Sometimes it was delicious and sometimes not so delicious. It continues to vary from year to year, of course; but it is never allowed to sink below a certain level of quality and a high level, at that. Twenty or thirty years ago it was sold almost exclusively in bulk, mostly to modest local cafés or to wine merchants who mixed it with whatever else was available and sold it as *vin ordinaire*. Not any more. Bustling machines possessed of an eerie dexterity now fill, cork and label the bottles. Massive trucks creep cautiously along the narrow track leading to the hamlet and load the crates. The most exigent restaurants in Paris await delivery. I don't remember that the Grand Véfour featured the wine from hereabouts in the epoch when I was briefly rich enough to dine there. I'm sure it does today. And the bottles go in their thousands to places a good deal further away than Paris. Growers regularly ship consigments to America, to England, to Scandinavia, to Japan, not to mention countries which not so long ago here they'd barely heard of—Australia, for example.

The whole business of wine-growing, in fact, has been transformed. With the exception of space shuttles and microprocessors, every conceivable mechanical and electronic device has invaded the countryside. When the vineyards were split up into tiny scattered patches everything had to be done manually with now and then a helping hoof from horses. Now that the patches have been amalgamated into holdings of ten or twelve hectares more modern methods are called for.

Every grower has a tractor, usually two or three. No one has his back and his spirit broken by having to yank for hours on a crankhandle as Maxime had to do. A touch on the starter of these monsters and off they go. They never break down, apparently. I wish they did. Their arrogant efficiency depresses me. I have a nostalgic feeling for that tottering contrivance which used to inspire Maxime's great profane cadenzas. There was something deeply touching about it. It was like a spavined old workhorse which could scarcely stagger up from the straw but which was determined to do its best to the end.

Huge mechanical monstrosities like something out of H.G. Wells's *War of the Worlds* lurch belligerently through the vineyards wrenching off bunches of grapes and, for all I know, spitting out any that aren't to their taste. About the only thing they aren't able to do, as far as I can tell, is to get together and sing choruses like the primitive human pickers I was accustomed to hear each night during the *vendange*. Marcel and a few other diehards persist in employing pickers but sooner or later they, too, will have to give in to the machines.

Unlike their fathers, the young men of the district have all attended oenological schools. They talk with intimidating authority about polymers and tartaric acid as they stoop over their test tubes. Their erudition has certainly contributed to improving the wine but I wish that the same improvement could have been brought about without having to make the cellars look like laboratories.

The old cellars were minute. Every time I entered Maxime's I cracked my head, Paul's was so small that it was overcrowded if more than four people were present. The vaulted roofs were stone, the floors were of tamped earth, the walls were garlanded with cobwebs. Everything else was wooden. The presses were made, as any god-fearing press should be, of solid oak. They looked as though they were of immense antiquity, and most of them were. Somehow they fitted into the decor, you felt they were almost members of the family, honorary grandmothers so to speak. I'd hate to have a grandmother anything like the brutish electronic devices which have taken over. They're housed in huge hangars where everything that isn't made of steel is made of aluminium. They ingurgitate the grapes when they're good and ready, they decide for themselves when to slow down and when to speed up, they don't require—and may even resent—any kind of human intervention. I daresay they'll eventually form their own union.

There was just one mechanical contraption which I was really fond of and so, naturally, it has now disappeared. This was the *alambic*, an ancient still of bizarre aspect composed of a wood-burning furnace, a copper cauldron, a tall chimney, twisted pipes, taps and drip-pans. It bore a striking resemblance to the sort of sculpture most admired by the ministers of newness. Mounted on wheels, it would trundle from village to village in the weeks following the *vendange*. The growers would bring along the mash left over from the pressing—not unlike adherents of some pagan cult bringing propitiatory offerings to their idol—and the master of the *alambic* would distil this into the merciless white brandy known as *marc*. The process stank horribly but the end product, once you got up the courage to face it, was delicious.

If the ministers of newness have anything to do with it, the preposterous sculptures will be around for a long time to come, although not, thank God, here; but we've seen the last of the *alambic*. Every winegrower formerly had the right to distil, a right transmitted from father to son. Rights, of course, are something which politicians, and especially socialist politicians, consider should be reserved to themselves so the peasants' right to distil was duly abrogated. It's remarkable how often the proponents of liberty decide that freedom is best served by imposing restrictions and prohibitions.

The *alambic* was banished, as far as I remember, at roughly the same time that washing-machines made their appearance. Previously, washing was done in a small pool on the outskirts of the hamlet which was fed by a cold pure stream. Sheets washed like this and laid out to dry on the grass smelt and felt better than any coroneted satin. The clanking robots that have moved in will never achieve anything like the same result.

Worse than this, the washing-machines have effectively sabotaged an important part of the social life of the community. Until they came along, the women of the hamlet collected once a week around the pool and, while pounding shirts and socks, had all the time in the world to exchange recipes, deplore the high cost of lamb chops and complain about their husbands' iniquities. Washing day was the rural equivalent of afternoon tea at the Ritz. Anybody who expects to find a sympathetic listener in a washing-machine is going to be bitterly disappointed.

For some of the changes that have occurred I myself have to shoulder the blame. The telephone, for instance, at any rate initially, was all my fault. I was what you might call the Alexander Graham Bell of the hamlet. When I had the telephone installed in the chateau the general view was that I was putting myself and everyone else at risk. Until then, the nearest telephone had been in Monsieur Boin's café, in other words a safe distance away. If it were to explode—and that was obviously bound to happen sooner or later—nobody in the hamlet was likely to be hurt. My telephone was a very different affair. Just let *that* explode and X-rays, electrical impulses and radiations could wipe out the entire population.

In the event of a major crisis, however—an ailing goat or grandmother, say, or an overdue delivery of oats—it was convenient to have access to a telephone without needing to saddle up and ride over to Monsieur Boin's. Not that anyone was going to run the risk of handling my telephone himself. Maxime wouldn't admit that he was scared but he was peremptory in ordering me to make calls on his behalf.

'You can telephone that *saloperie de forgeron* for me and tell him . . . '

'There's the phone, Maxime, help yourself.'

'How do you expect me to ring up, *pauvre crétin*? Do I know how it works, your telegraph or wireless or Morse code or whatever it is?'

'There's no mystery. Pick up the receiver, turn the handle, wait until the operator answers and that's it.'

'And what do you want me to say to your *putain de téléphoniste*? I've never even met her. You just ring up the blacksmith, as I tell you . . . '

146

Telephones are not looked on as a hazard nowadays. There's one (or two or three) in every house. Maxime himself, when disinclined to walk across the road, doesn't hesitate to call me up simply in order to have a chat . . .

I have to take responsibility, too, for replacing the vigorous xenophobia which used to prevail with a wishy-washy tolerance. I don't mean that I won everyone over with my quiet charm and amusing conversation so that they were completely reconciled to foreigners. It would be more accurate to say that I broke them down by sheer weight of numbers. Obviously, I had Australian friends coming to stay from time to time and a broadminded view was taken of this by my neighbours. If you were fool enough to be born an Australian, then it was natural enough to consort from time to time with your fellow outcasts. But I went further. There have also been (I've just totted them up) American, Greek, Italian, German, English, Egyptian, Russian (red and white), Samoan, New Zealand, Swedish, Scottish, Israeli, South African, Slovene, Belgian and Dutch visitors. Parisians, too. In the end, my neighbours grew accustomed to the irruption of these freaks of nature. I did worry a little about the possible reaction in the hamlet when I invited a black American girl to spend a few days with us. But no; she was a big success. For years after she came here, 'What's the news,' Maxime would ask, 'of your *belle blonde*?'

The consequence is that foreigners are now taken for granted. You'd have to be an Uzbek or an Inuit to attract a second glance. Japanese wander around our old hill town peering anxiously into their view-finders. A German family has installed itself within a few kilometres of the hamlet and half the farmhands (because nowadays everyone has at least a couple of workers) are Italian or Portuguese or Vietnamese. There are even Parisians strolling around unharmed. I never thought I'd see Parisians treated just as if they were people like anyone else.

With the barbarians have come barbarous habits and once again I was the first to sin. Very, very sporadically indeed, some occasion or other—as it might be, the birth of a male grandchild or the death of an old enemy—would be judged of such exceptional importance that it merited something less commonplace than a glass of wine. It was then, I discovered, that a bottle of whisky would be brought out, possibly for the first time in five or ten years. It was daunting stuff. 'Blackhead Scotch Whisky', you'd read on the label, 'Genuine Old Gin brewed in Saigon from selected hops by Grimoire & Fils, Wholesale Grocers and Paint Merchants'. The assembled guests, all of them endowed with highly trained palates, would gallantly gulp it down with civil murmurs of delight and every appearance of nausea.

I hated to see them suffer. What could be done about it? If whisky had to be drunk, I finally decided, I could at least deliver them from the misery of swilling the concoction stirred up in the vats of Monsieur Grimoire and Son. It was in this charitable spirit that I introduced my neighbours to pure malt. They took to it instantaneously, not merely as an alternative to Blackhead but with genuine appreciation. Malt whisky has become a favoured drink hereabouts. I don't know whether to be glad or sorry. As a surly old reactionary, I feel remorseful at having unsettled local tradition. Against this, it's nice to know that I will have made fools of the scholars. I won't be around to snigger but I feel an anticipatory pleasure at the thought that in a hundred years or so archaeologists will be digging up malt whisky bottles and using them as proof that the Berry was once invaded by hordes of whisky-inflamed Celts.

You can get the stuff now in the local supermarket. Because (although this time I had nothing to do with it) a supermarket has been opened up no great distance away. It has had a profoundly deleterious effect on shopping habits. I used to see housewives scrutinising veal cutlets or Brussels sprouts with commendable suspicion before deciding to buy. They chose leeks or tomatoes with the overt mistrustfulness of diamond merchants. Nowadays they'll buy prepackaged meat and deep-frozen beans without a qualm. Peanut butter, which the old lady who ran our general store believed to be a whimsical invention of mine, can be purchased, and is purchased, as readily as sweetcorn and compact discs.

Our three village shops have not yet gone under and this is something of a miracle. There are hundreds perhaps thousands of villages in France where not even a bakery remains. The supermarket has already eradicated a number of shops in our neighbouring villages. Needless to say, its brisk shopgirls don't offer you a glass of wine (you'll be lucky if you get a '*Bonjour*' out of them) any more than they're inclined to waste their time discussing old Madame Dulac's dropsy or Monsieur Grandval's wife's quarrel with the Mayor's second cousin three times removed.

But social life was doomed to suffer with the evolution of the economy. A holding of one or two hectares might not have brought in enough to buy washing-machines and similar gadgets but you could live on it and have some time left over. Looking after ten or twelve hectares of vines means a ten-hour or twelve-hour day—thirteen or fourteen in the summer. Clients are likely to drop in and hang around interminably. Trucks are waiting to be loaded. The paperwork is piling up. The official view is that it might be possible to make wine without grapes but certainly not without forms—tax returns, wage slips, declarations of production figures, authorisations, lists of regulations, schedules, reports, certificates . . . They don't leave any room for our weekly tours of the village. Just once a year—on New Year's Day—we go in a body from house to house was we did in the past once a week. Bureaucracy has gobbled up the hours which we devoted to convivial talk and clinking of glasses.

My neighbours used to be poor. No one went hungry but no one had any money to spare. In no way thanks to the bureaucrats, they've become prosperous. They've earned their prosperity. This, at any rate, is one change I'm more than ready to rejoice in. At long last, people can afford to go off on holiday, to dine in good restaurants. The old houses have been smartened up, inside and out. My chateau is no longer an object of wonder. Every household is now equipped with central heating and running water and bathrooms and electricity and all the other marvels which formerly I alone possessed.

Once upon a time I was the local plutocrat. From my point of view, that's the most radical change which has occurred. I've replaced Le Biguin as far and away the shabbiest member of the community. His poverty never seemed to worry him. It did me. I was guiltily conscious of the gap between his income and mine. If poor old Biguin were still alive the gap would be more pronounced than ever. His bank balance would be immeasurably sturdier than mine.

I was also the only owner of a car for miles around. I'm still the only owner of *a* car: all my neighbours have two or three. For their sakes, I'm delighted. Cars have made their lives much easier. They've done nothing, however, to promote human contact. In prehistoric times when everyone either walked or drove a horse-drawn cart, neighbours would meet on the road, stop for a yarn and probably end up drinking a glass of wine in whoever's cellar was nearest. You can't enjoy the same camaraderie while whizzing past each other in cars.

Changes drove me out of Paris. They have not driven me from my hamlet. It remains an enclave of civilisation. No glass pyramids are envisaged. Apart from the freshly painted houses and the asphalt surface on the little road, nothing much has altered externally. I look out on the same vine-covered hillsides.

I'm not sure that even a glass pyramid would induce me to leave. My friends are still across the way and none of them has changed. I had good friends in Paris, too—Pierre and Alain and Jacques and . . . But seeing them had come to pose logistical problems. The pace of life had changed too much. Wednesday would suit Pierre but not me; I was free on Sunday but Alain was busy; Jacques had shifted to the suburbs. A week of telephone calls was needed to arrange a meeting, then more telephone calls to change the day, the hour, the meeting-place.

We don't have to telephone each other here in the hamlet. I give no warning before making a nuisance of myself to Paul and Jean-Marc, I don't wait for an invitation before dropping in on Maxime or anyone else for a glass of wine. We may not meet as often but when we do get together the old conviviality prevails, the old sagas are recited with the old verve and embellishments. And the old solidarity is intact. I know, we all know, that everyone will respond automatically to an emergency. I need no convincing that coming to this special corner of France was one of my rare intelligent decisions. I've become less exclusive, though. The friends to whom I owe so much contentment and reassurance, so much help and laughter now include some who live as far as fifteen kilometres away. But I don't think I'll bother to look any further than that.

So the moment has come to borrow that monumental glass from which I took my first drink with Maxime, to fill it to the brim with the perfect wine of this perfect region and to drink a health to Maxime and Suzanne, to Paul and Germaine, Jean-Marc and Martine, Alain and Dominique, Roger and Suzanne, Dominique and Isabelle (not the old lady I thought might be a witch), Régis and Liliane, Claude and Geneviève, the other Claude, my staunch printer friend, and Viviane, Dédé and Thérèse, the two Pascals, Raymonde, Marcel and Huguette, Raymond and Odette. *A la votre, mes amis—et merci*!

Inside Outside

ANDREW RIEMER

ON A FREEZING NOVEMBER DAY IN 1946, ANDREW Riemer, then a ten-year-old with mumps, left a bomb-scarred Budapest on his way to Australia. A few days before Christmas in 1990 he returned to the city of his birth where, amid the decay of a world waking from totalitarian rule, he tried to reconstruct the past from shreds of memory and family myth.

In the years between, his career had taken him from being an expert in French-knitting, a skill acquired when, unable to speak English, he was put in a class for intellectually handicapped children, to Sydney University, where he now teaches English Literature.

Andrew Riemer has written a classic. Witty, lucid, heartrending and wonderfully funny. No reader will ever forget his two worlds, or the profound questions he asks about them.
JILL KER CONWAY

The Habsburg Café

ANDREW RIEMER

REVISITING EASTERN EUROPE, HAVING LEFT IT AT THE AGE of ten, award-winning author Andrew Riemer presents a sparkling account of his travels in Austria and Hungary, the heartland of the Habsburg Empire. He takes us from Vienna, which he calls a theme park dedicated to images of a romantic past, to the chaos of contemporary Hungary. The cities and towns of his childhood memories have altered almost beyond recognition and yet are somehow familiar, with the spirit of the long-dead Habsburg world evident — the cafés are still filled with cakes oozing cream and custard, and the rich aroma of freshly roasted coffee and vanilla.

A travel book, an exploration of the past and a shrewd examination of contemporary politics and culture, *The Habsburg Café* illuminates the experiences of a troubled and perplexing age.

Out From The Past

Tim Baker

IN THIS COLLECTION OF TWELVE SHORT STORIES, SET IN Europe and Australia, the author's range of perspective is broad — he moves easily from the story of a widower coming to terms with his new life to that of two young Australian boys trapped in a violent storm at sea. Suspense is cleverly built up, often with unexpected results, which makes *Out From the Past* writing at its powerful best.

Tim Baker writes poetically and is, without doubt, a major new talent on the Australian literary scene.

These short stories ... exemplify the best of writing.
William Wharton, author of *Birdy*